Marlinspike
Sailor's
Knots and
Crafts

Marlinspike Sailor's Knots and Crafts

A Step-by-Step Guide to Tying Classic Sailor's Knots to Create, Adorn, and Show Off

Barbara Merry

INTERNATIONAL MARINE / McGRAW-HILL EDUCATION
Camden, Maine • New York • Chicago • San Francisco
Lisbon • London • Madrid • Mexico City • Milan • New Delhi
San Juan • Seoul • Singapore • Sydney • Toronto

To my granddaughter.

1 2 3 4 5 6 7 8 9 10 11 12 13 14 15 QVS/QVS 1 9 8 7 6 5 4 3
ISBN 978-0-07-178998-1
MHID 0-07-178998-7
Ebook ISBN 0-07-178998-7

**Library of Congress Cataloging-in-Publication Data is available
from the Library of Congress.**

International Marine/McGraw-Hill Education books are available at special
quantity discounts to use as premiums and sales promotions or for use in
corporate training programs. To contact a representative, please e-mail us
at bulksales@mcgraw-hill.com.

This book is printed on acid-free paper.

Questions regarding the content of this book should be addressed to
www.internationalmarine.com

Questions regarding the ordering of this book should be addressed to
McGraw-Hill Education
Customer Service Department
P.O. Box 547
Blacklick, OH 43004
Retail customers: 1-800-262-4729
Bookstores: 1-800-722-4726

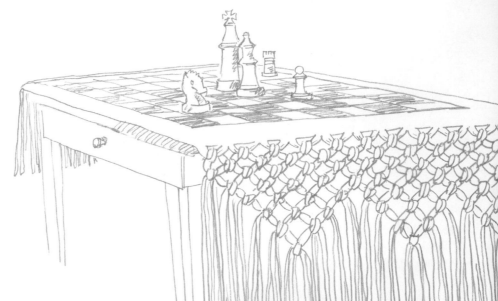

Contents

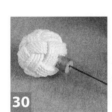

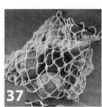

Introduction

This book is based on the principles of marlinspike seamanship, a term used in the marine trades to describe rope work, wire work, and knots. Sailors use practical marlinspike seamanship skills to make, customize, or fix a boat's running rigging, anchor lines, docklines, and other ropes and wires used to operate a boat and keep the crew safe.

Sailors also use their marlinspike seamanship skills to make decorative items, called "fanciwork." A sailor might employ fanciwork to decorate his ditty bag or sea chest. He or she might tie a wide, flat sennit (braid), or a series of knots to serve as a lanyard for a belt or knife, or tie a decorative flat knot to use as a trivet or doormat.

Earth-Friendly Shellacking

When it was first suggested to me that I write an earth-friendly knot book, I thought to myself, *how easy*! Knot tyers the world over have been demonstrating their skills for hundreds of years in leather, cotton, hemp, and colorful silks. However, one small but important part of knot tying almost stopped me in my quest: what to use for glue and coating? I've always loved shellac, but how could I get around the use of denatured alcohol? What did the artisans of old use in place of the toxic stuff? I realized that I needed to use a different form of alcohol. Feeling a little weird, I explained what I was searching for to the first clerk in the first liquor store I happened upon. Nancy Laboissonniere listened to me carefully, and when I finished my story she stepped from around the counter and disappeared down the aisle, a moment later returning with a bottle of pure grain alcohol in her fist.

"This will do it," she explained.

All I could say was "Wow, how do you know this?"

"I have a masters degree in clinical laboratory science from the University of Rhode Island," she answered.

I'm delighted to report that grain alcohol works better than denatured alcohol for dissolving the shellac flakes.

Grain alcohol can be used instead of denatured alcohol when working with shellac flakes, making the entire process much more enjoyable.

The overhand knot is the most common knot and serves as the base for many more complex knots.

The square knot has many practical purposes.

What I call a package knot is kind of a nick name. The sailors (and others in the trade) tie the first part of the square knot with an extra turn–that way one can tie the rest of the square knot without asking someone to hold it with their finger so it won't slip. The package knot is a binding knot. A true package knot is tied completely differently.

If you look around, you will see knots everywhere and tied into all sorts of strings and ropes: the overhand knot used for sewing, the bow knot used to tie shoelaces, the square knot used to bundle newspapers or branches for recycling. This book focuses on using simple knots such as these to make both practical and decorative projects.

We start the book with two basic knots, the Turk's Head knot (described in Chapter 1) and the square knot (described in Chapter 2). Square knotting might bring back memories of 1960s crafts or Boy Scout or Girl Scout projects. Those who have served on maritime duty might know the square knot as the one used in McNamara's lace. The square knot with a minor manipulation turns into a surgeon's knot. The Ashley's knot #2216 is a highly decorative knot. You'd want to use it as a knob covering—perhaps a gearshift knob or a knob at the end of a tiller. This knot is described in Chapter 3.

Overhand knots arranged in a special way turn into a trucker's hitch that will hold a bundle of branches effortlessly. The overhand knot is also the starter knot for netting, described in Chapter 5.

There is a saying that perfectly reflects the theme of this book: "What's old is new again." All knots begin with a piece of rope or cordage, and Chapter 9 explains how to make rope and how to use this homemade rope in several projects. (See the Choosing Cordage section in this chapter for advice on purchasing cordage.) Ropes and cordage have been made like this since the time of the Pharaohs. Lengths of cordage or rope twisted from papyrus fibers have been found in Egyptian tombs. Shellac, used as a coating in some of the projects in this book, was used as a finish for wooden items in China since the time of the Emperor Tang.

Many of you will recognize the patterns that I used for the projects in this book. My variations on these patterns include a small ocean plat knot sewn to embroidered canvas to make an eyeglass case (Chapter 7). I also created an Altoids tin cover based on a cigarette case pattern from the *Encyclopedia of Knots* (Chapter 2), which I couldn't have done without the help of another knot tyer, Marty Casey. I'm awfully proud of the rope hammock as well (Chapter 13). Hammocks that are tied rather than woven are usually really uncomfortable, but my hammock is both lovely to look at and comfortable to lie in.

I think you'll find that this book covers the basics, with projects for young and old and the expert or novice knot tyer. All the projects are handsome and useful in an earth-friendly way.

NOTE: By no means do these projects demand cotton, leather, manila, or rayon. They can be easily tied in corresponding-size synthetic material. Use the flame from a lighter to fuse the ends of synthetic cordage. Instant glue from the tube will hold ends together nicely, and a coating of polyurethane will harden, seal, and add shine to your work, if desired.

Choosing Cordage

I think just about the best thing in the world is to curl up with a good book. I like the real kind–carefully crafted with hard covers front and back, nice paper pages, and easy-to-read print. But I also love my e-reader. Almost every evening before I go to sleep, I prop it up right in front of me and turn the pages with just a light push. Reading the printed word in either format makes me happy and content.

I feel the same way about today's cordage—thankful for the long-standing natural material and simultaneously appreciative of the possibilities offered by the new materials. In Chapter 5 I focus on projects from the net knot, for example. I'd use a natural fiber to make the net knot string shopping bag. Isn't that the idea—to replace the plastic ones? But if I used the bag to carry clothes to and from the laundromat, I'd make it from synthetic cordage, which is tough, light, and quick-drying. It's nice that we have a choice between natural and synthetic cordage, because it hasn't always been the case; synthetic cordage first appeared in 1938.

Cordage is as elegant as it is simple. Groups of individually twisted strands are themselves twisted around one another in the opposite direction. The finished product is a bundle of interlocking tension, with each strand holding another in check and keeping the entire rope from unraveling.

The quality of the cordage depends on the number of levels of interlocking twists, the quality of the fundamental material (the length of the "staple" in natural cordage, and the chemical makeup of synthetic cordage), the consideration given to twist tension (or braid), and whether the cordage is finished properly. Synthetic cordage is heat set—the last step after the cordage is twisted is passing it through an oven. Other cordage is often coated with a wax or, in the case of natural fiber ropes or twines designed for uses on a farm, often impregnated with rodent repellent. Interesting enough, special synthetic rope designed to be used in trucking is impregnated with chemicals that repel UV rays.

Naturally, cordage made with more care costs more. I hope that all who decide to purchase cordage for a project in this book will not use cheap or used string. Even the most skilled knot tyers are doomed and destined to produce a less than perfect result if they choose poor quality cordage.

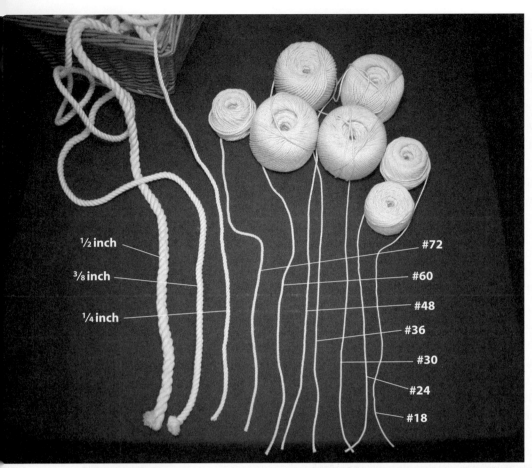

½ inch
⅜ inch
¼ inch

#72
#60
#48
#36
#30
#24
#18

Understanding Materials and Measurements

Here are the two "M"s of cordage for projects in this book: material and measurements.

These are the materials I used to make different projects in this book:

> I use cotton in the seine twine and cotton rope projects, including net knot bags (Chapter 5), monkey's fist projects (Chapter 4), and square knot projects (Chapter 2).

> I use manila (also called abaca) in doormats (Chapter 7).

> I use cotton rope for the companionway stair treads (Chapter 7).

> I use rayon and leather to make the knotted jewelry in Chapter 10.

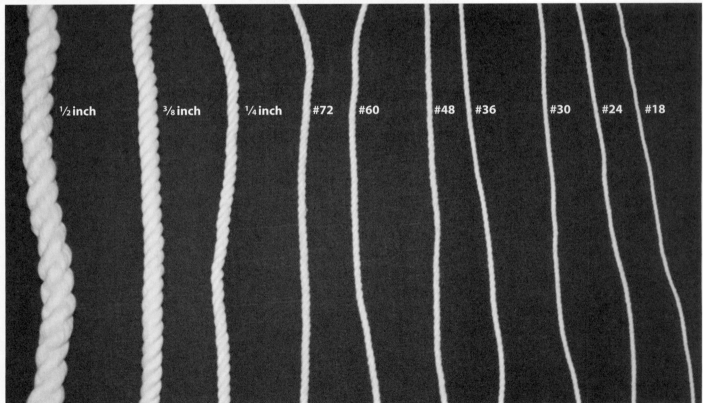

½ inch   ⅜ inch   ¼ inch   #72   #60   #48   #36   #30   #24   #18

Thinner cotton seine twine is measured by the number of threads it contains. Shown here is cotton seine twine from #18 up to #72. Thicker cotton rope is measured in inches, shown here from ¼ inch up to ½ inch.

Measurement information holds true for either natural or synthetic cordage. For our purpose let's examine a favorite of mine, #48 cotton seine twine. The "48" means that it is made of 48 threads of cotton. The #18 cotton seine twine is about half as big, and the #84 cotton seine twine is twice as big as #48 cotton seine twine. After #120, cotton seine twine measurements "morph" into inches, and cotton seine twine becomes cotton rope. For the sake of simplicity, I chose projects using manila (abaca) fibers in rope form because projects using this stuff are measured in inches. Also, be aware that cotton rope is very expensive—so the knot tyer will want to take this into account. Can he or she execute the project in the less expensive (but still natural) fiber rather than out of the very expensive cotton rope?

If you choose to craft your project from one of the natural fiber ropes, you'll need to protect it from damp, mold, mildew, and small rodents. If you make the ditty bag out of canvas (see Chapter 13), you'll also need to protect your project from chafe. Any bag rubbing against woodwork or a cabin bulkhead in time will become worn in that spot.

Projects made from synthetic seine twine or rope are generally impervious to damp, mold, mildew, and small rodents. For the most part, synthetic stuff is tough and will hold up well.

Sources of Materials

I purchase my materials from the following places of business. Foremost in my mind are these criteria: value for my dollar, availability of the product, consistency of the product, customer service, and the company's knowledge of the product.

Wilcox Marine Supply
30 Wilcox Road
Stonington, CT 06378
(860)536-4206
My favorite, a family owned business.

R and W Enterprises
http://rwrope.com/

Memphis Net and Twine
http://www.memphisnet.net/

La Stella Celeste, Inc.
5130 Abel Lane
Jacksonville, FL 32254
http://stellaceleste.com

(Rayon Supplier)
www.satincord.com
1-888-728-8245

Finish Supplies
www.shellac.net
Good quality, nice people, too.

Tandy Leather
http://www.tandyleatherfactory.com/

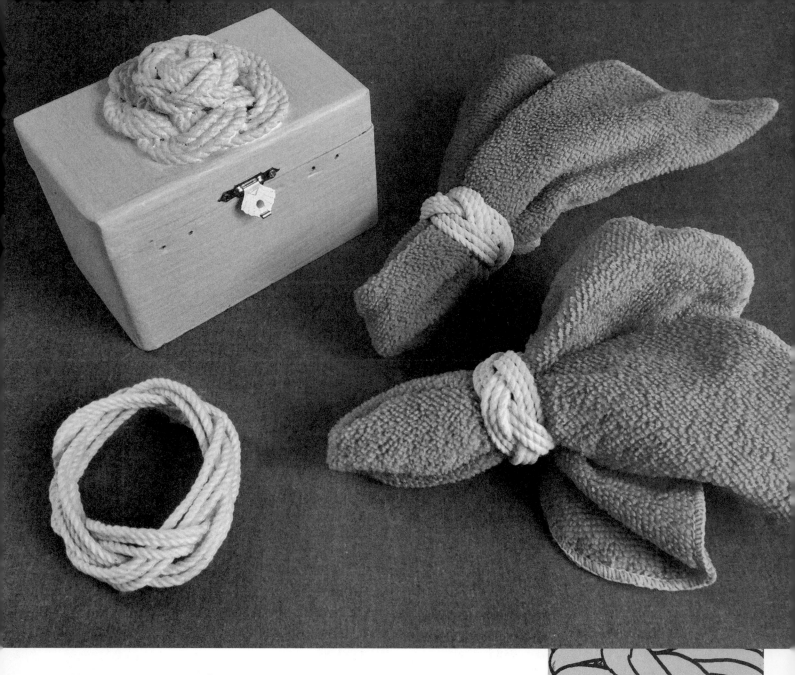

CHAPTER 1 > *Projects from the*
Turk's Head Knot

Sailors will recognize the Turk's Head knot as the one traditionally tied to the spot on the wheel where the rudder is centered. This knot can also be found on bell pulls, stanchions, and a tiller. First tied as a practical knot, the Turk's Head knot was often meant to keep the feet from slipping, as when tied into the bolt ropes on bowsprit netting.

The Turk's Head knot came into prominence during the era of the tall-masted sailing ships. The knot was tied in many different configurations, often around a spar or mast to mark the sailor's path through the maze of rigging to his station. Today, the Turk's Head knot is a popular choice for decorative knotting projects.

The Turk's Head knot is a series of loops (also known as bights or clovers) braided together to create texture and visual interest. These knots can be made directly around a cylindrical object such as a stanchion, or they can be made on a table and then either used as a mat or tightened around a cylinder (to create a bracelet, for example).

The projects in this chapter use Turk's Head knots made on a table. This chapter explains how to create Turk's Head knots this way. Chapter 8 explains how to tie a Turk's Head knot around a cylindrical object (decorative hitching).

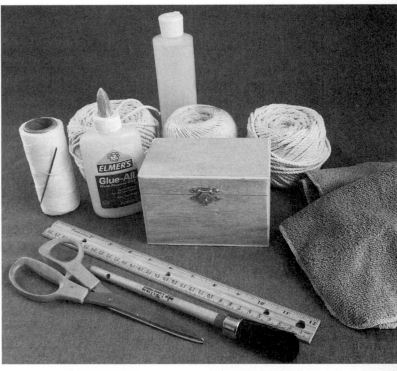

Gather these simple materials to create nautical napkin rings and a box with a nautical motif, perfect as a gift or recipe box with flair.

Napkin Ring

5 feet of #48 cotton seine twine
1 to 2 feet of thread and a needle
sharp knife or scissors
ruler

Each of the thousand-plus different kinds of Turk's Heads has a numbered title. The one we're tying here is the simplest. The width of the braid is given in the number of "leads," and the rounded parts (which look like clovers) are known as "bights." It's labeled 3L x 4B (3 leads and 4 bights).

It helps to tape or pin the outer edge of each clover to your work surface as you make each clover.

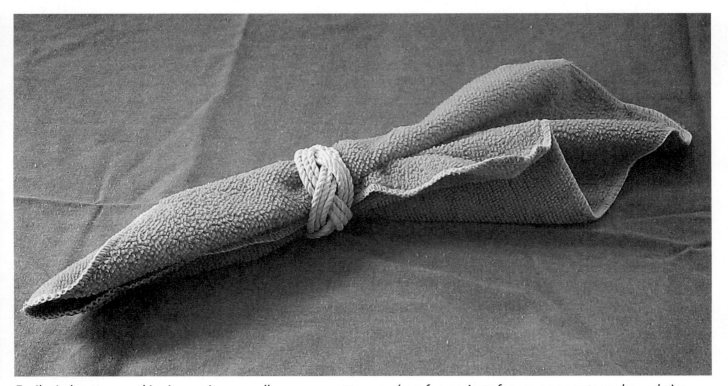

Easily tied, cotton napkin rings suit your galley or your cottage and are fun projects for young ones to make and give.

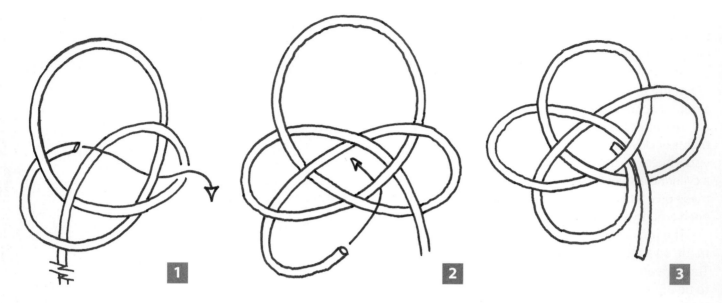

1. Making the first, second, and third bights. 2. Tying in the fourth bight. 3. The final napkin ring has three lines laid, so two more should be added—here we are just starting to lay in the second.

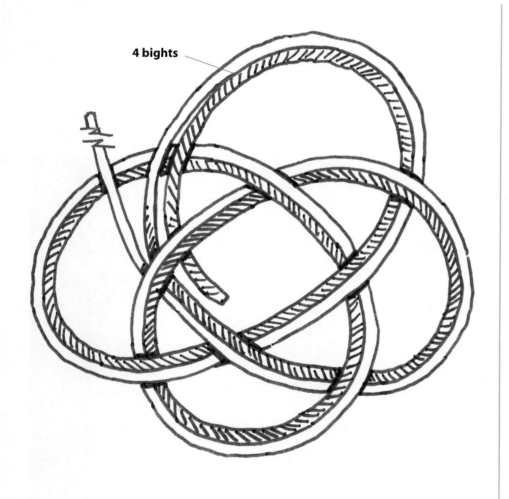

4 bights

Here the third and final line is being laid.

Follow these steps and refer to the drawings to make the napkin ring:

1 › Lay the twine out on a table. About a foot from the right-hand end of the twine, make two overlapping bights (loops) about 2 inches in diameter with the twine. The longer end of the twine is the working end, and the shorter end of the twine is the bitter end.

2 › Weave the working end under and over the two bights to create a third clover. Cross the bitter end over the working end to begin a fourth bight.

3 › Move the bitter end to the top left, and lay the working end against it to complete the fourth bight.

4 › Using the first strand as a model, continue to lay the working end along all four bights, threading the working end under and over the bights as needed.

5 › Use the working end of the twine to make the third and final strand.

6 > Put a 1-inch- to 2-inch-diameter cylinder (such as a spool or a piece of dowel) in the middle of the knot where the four cloves intersect. Untape or unpin the clovers and gently pull on the strands to both tighten and remove all the slack.

7 > Sew the bitter end and the working end into the other three leads. Trim off the extra cordage next to the sewn end.

8 > Remove the completed napkin ring from the cylinder when you are done.

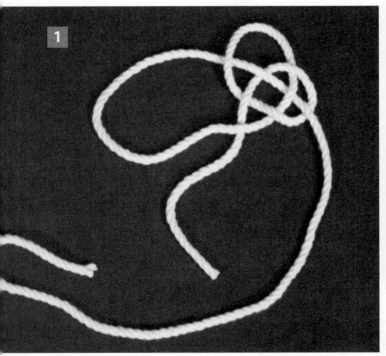

Three bights made for the napkin ring.

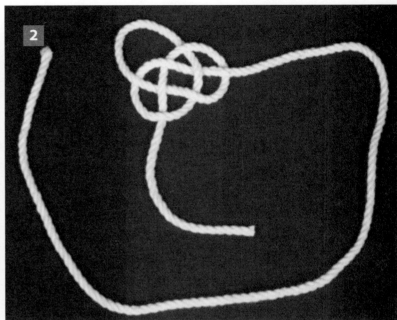

Two bights made for the napkin ring.

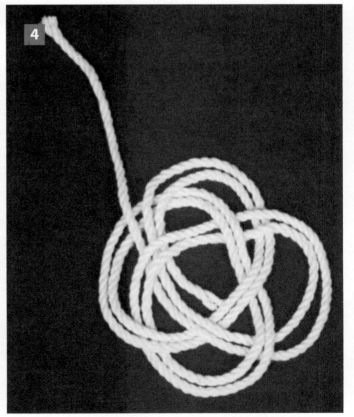

While at times when tying you might feel like you are piling up spaghetti, there really is some order to how this Turk's Head is tied.

Four bights completed for the napkin ring.

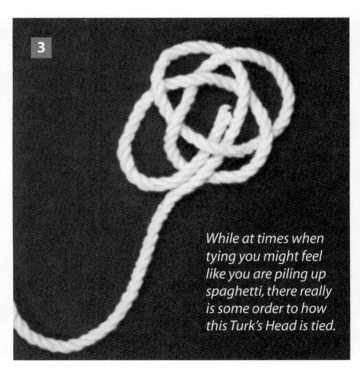

Beginning the second lead around the bights.

The first two leads are complete and the third lead is being made with the working end, shown going up to the left.

The third and final lead is being laid down.

bight

three leads

3L × 5B

The finished Turk's Head bracelet. Note that cotton twine can shrink, so make the bracelet a bit larger than your wrist if you are going to be swimming or showering with it on.

Turk's Head Bracelet

10 feet of #48 cotton seine twine
1 to 2 feet of heavy thread and
a needle
sharp knife or scissors
ruler

This is the next most complicated Turk's Head knot. It's labeled 3L x 5B (which means 3 leads and 5 bights). It makes a nice mat knot, and after some manipulation it can be turned into the Turk's Head bracelet.

The knot is easier to make if you tape or pin each clover to your work surface as you make it. Follow these steps and refer to the drawings to make a Turk's Head bracelet.

1 ► About 6 inches from the bitter end of the twine, make two overlapping bights to create the first two clovers.

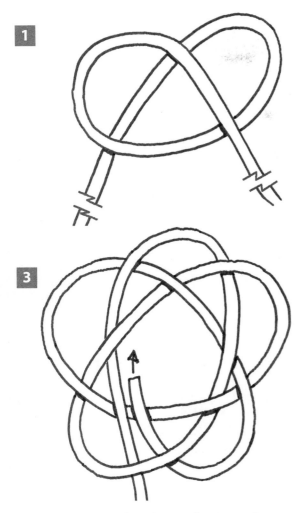

Creating the 5 bights—after the two leads are done, as shown here, add the third (not shown).

2> Make the third bight, weaving the twine over and under the other two clovers.

3> Add the last bight for the bracelet.

4> Lay a second line of twine against the first, using the first lay as a guide. Then lay a third line of twine against the first two lines to complete the bracelet.

5> Put enough slack in your work so you can place a cylinder that is the diameter you want for the bracelet (such as a water glass or a wide dowel) in the center of the knot.

6> Flip the sides of the knot up along the glass or dowel, and tighten the knot against the cylinder by pulling gently on the bights.

7> Sew the working end and the bitter end of the twine to the bracelet. Trim the cordage near the sewn ends.

8> Slide the finished bracelet off the cylinder and flip the bracelet inside out to hide where you sewed the ends.

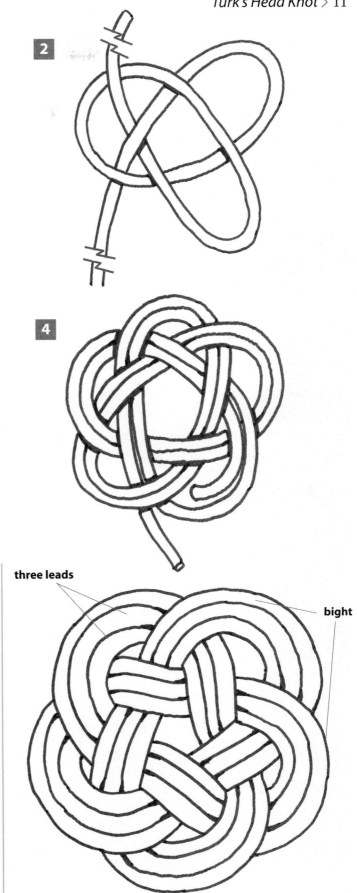

The third lead has been threaded into the five bights.

Decorated Wooden Box

4 inch by 2 inch by 2 inch unfinished wooden box
2 to 3 feet of #18 cotton seine twine
3 feet of #36 cotton seine twine
2 to 3 feet of #48 cotton seine twine
5 to 6 feet of #60 cotton seine twine
scissors or sharp knife
ruler
white glue
masking tape
shellac and brush

One possibility for the decorations on the top of the wooden box uses multiple Turk's Head knots shown from the top left: a 2L x 5B, another 2L x 5B, a 3L x 5B (like the napkin ring just tied), and another 3L x 5 B.

An inexpensive wooden box, readily available at crafts stores, can be made attractive and nautical with the addition of four Turk's Head knot variations.

A fun and family-friendly project, this decorated wooden box looks like an elaborate project, but it is built up from a number of simple knots (see Chapter 9 for another decorated wooden box). Unfinished boxes are available from crafts stores everywhere. The box pictured is 4 inches by 2 inches by 2 inches and has four knots stacked on it.

Use the Turk's Head knot-tying skills you developed in the napkin ring and bracelet projects to make a set of knots to stack on top of the wooden box.

Follow these steps to create the box shown in the accompanying photos.

1 › Stain or paint the box according to the manufacturer's directions.

2 › While the box is drying, make these four Turk's Head knots:

- 2L x 5B (2 leads and 5 bights) Turk's Head knot tied with 2 to 3 feet of #18 cotton seine twine
- 2L x 5B Turk's Head knot tied with 3 feet of #36 cotton seine twine
- 3L x 5B (3 leads and 5 bights) Turk's Head knot tied with 2 to 3 feet of #48 cotton seine twine
- 3L x 5B Turk's Head knot tied with 5 to 6 feet of #60 cotton seine twine

3> Arrange the four knots as shown, nested together like Russian Matryoshka dolls. The different knots, tied in various twine sizes, will fit nicely: the #18, the smallest, fits inside the #36, which fits into the #48. The three "nested" knots now fit atop the #60 Turk's Head mat.

4> Glue all the knots in place and then glue the stack of knots to the top of the box. (Thin the glue with a little water and apply with a small watercolor brush.)

5> Finish the box with more shellac, stain, or paint as needed.

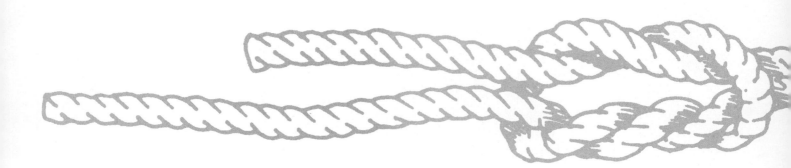

CHAPTER 2 > *Projects from the*
Square Knot

The Square Knot

The overhand knot is the easiest knot to tie, tied in a single strand. The square knot tied in two strands.

The square knot projects take minimal materials yet yield marvelous results.

A square knot.

The square knot morphed from a humble working knot into an art form in the court of Queen Anne of England. The ladies of her court would tie intricate patterns of square knots in the fringe of woven material. The knot enjoyed popularity in France under the name that many know today: macramé. The craft found its way onto ships during the whaling era and once again underwent a name change at the hands of the whalers, who dubbed it a square knot.

To tie a square knot, follow these steps:

1 > Lay two pieces of twine parallel to each other.

2 > Thread the bottom piece of twine over, under, and over the top piece of twine, forming a half-knot.

3 > Pick up the two pieces of twine that are now at the top of your work area and cross them over, under, and over each other in the same pattern as the bottom pieces.

4 > A square knot is formed. Pull the left and right ends of the twine to tighten the knot.

With a square knot, the pieces of twine on either side of the completed knot are parallel to each other, lying either above or below the loop of twine. If they are not parallel (for example, on the left side of the knot one piece of twine lies above the loop and the other lies beneath it), then you can wind up with a knot called a granny knot.

Dog Collar

about 12 feet (see Note) of #48 cotton seine
twine
dog collar clip
corkboard or like material with T pins, or
clipboard
scissors or sharp knife
superglue
ruler

Note: This collar is $5/8$ inch wide by 10 to 12 inches long. To ensure that the collar will fit your dog, you will want to determine the shrinkage of the cotton material you are using. Different cordage by different manufacturers will shrink differently. In order to discover this factor for your material, cut a 12-inch piece, dip it in very hot water, and let it dry. Measure once more to determine the amount of shrinkage, and factor this into the length of the collar.

This project fits a medium-sized dog, such as a cocker spaniel, border collie, or larger terrier.

To attach the twine to either end of the clip, follow these steps:

1 > Middle (fold in half) the 12-foot piece of #48 cotton seine twine.

2 > Attach the middled twine to one end of the plastic clip with a lark's head knot/cow hitch. Take an extra turn around the bar with both of the strands to make the knot thicker (see drawing on page 16 for guidance on how to make the knot).

A dog collar is a fast and fun project—one to build your confidence.

Attaching the twine to each of the collar clips.

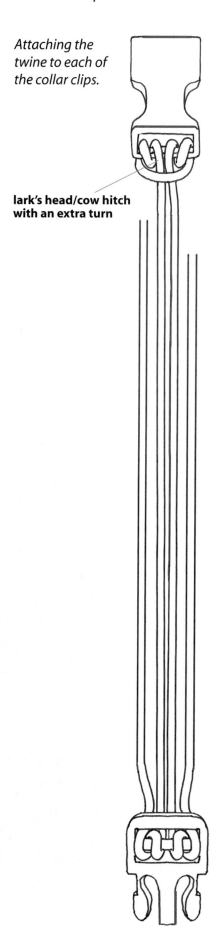

lark's head/cow hitch with an extra turn

3> Bring the two strands down to the other end of the clip. After making sure the length is right for your dog's neck, take two turns around the bar of the clip with each strand, as shown below.

This is now the core of your dog collar.

4> Arrange the two halves of the clips facing away from each other. Take the two loose ends and tie a chain of square knots that encompass the two core strands. Continue until you reach the clip at the other end.

5> Cut the ends off close to your work and glue them with superglue.

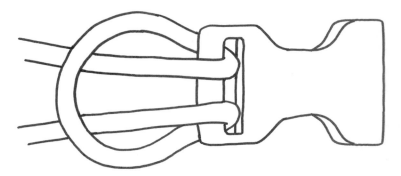

Twine attached to dog collar clip with a lark's head knot (also known as a cow hitch).

Extra turn added to lark's head knot to thicken the knot.

Square knots on dog collar almost complete.

Decorated Carafe

standard glass carafe
150 feet of #48 cotton seine twine
sharp knife or scissors
ruler
masking tape

This project uses lark's head knots, square knots, and clove hitches to decorate a glass carafe.

Follow these steps to start the project:

1> Cut a 6-foot length of #48 cotton seine twine. This will be your base cord.

2> Cut 24 pieces of #48 cotton seine twine that are each 72 inches long.

3> Middle (fold in half) each of the 72-inch strands.

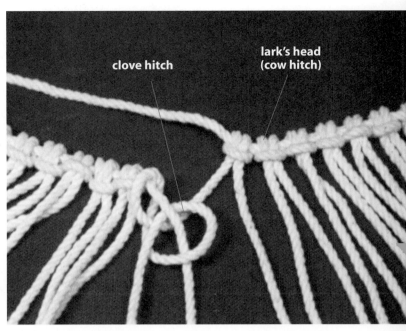

On the right: adding lark's head knots to the base cord.

A completed glass carafe.

Carafe with base cord wrapped around its neck.

Clove hitch knot.

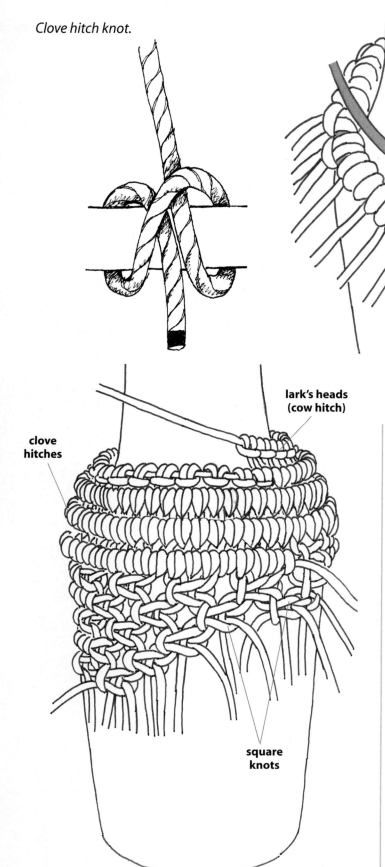

Start the clove hitches on the second row.

clove
hitches

lark's heads
(cow hitch)

square
knots

Square knots tied on the strands all the way to the bottom of the carafe.

Then attach each strand to the base cord using a lark's head knot (also known as a cow hitch).

Next, add clove hitches to the project by following these steps:

1 > Pick up your "hula skirt" of strands (you will have 48 strands—the 24 lark's head strands tied to the base cord—hanging from the base cord) and wrap it around the neck of the carafe. Tape the short end of the base cord to the glass.

2 > If the wine carafe is larger or smaller, you will have to add or subtract the knotted-on strands from it so that they encircle the neck of the carafe. To execute the pattern, though, the number of strands hanging from the base cord must be divisible by four.

3 > Pick up the first strand attached to the base cord and tie a clove hitch with it (the knot is illustrated above). Pull all the slack out of this first hitch and repeat with the following 47 strands.

4 > Continue hitching until you've completed three rows of clove hitches.

5 > Tuck the base cord up and out of the way. You'll be using it again at the end of the project.

Now you need to change to square knotting. Tie square knots in the strands down to the bottom of the bottle, following the pattern described in the Altoids tin cover instructions later in this chapter.

The last part of the project is finishing the bottom of the carafe. This serves two purposes: to prevent the covering from slipping up the glass, and to add a nice pattern that repeats the hitching on the top of the carafe. Follow these steps:

1> Pick up the base cord that you had tucked aside and weave it down to the bottom of the square knotting.

2> Use the base cord to encircle the bottom of the carafe, and then tie off the base cord.

3> Use the strands to tie one last row of clove hitches to the base cord.

Altoids Tin Knotted Cover

13 feet of #30 dark-color cotton seine twine (optional)
60 feet of #30 natural-color cotton seine twine
corkboard or like material with T pins
scissors or sharp knife
ruler

This is a useful and pretty project. The empty tin will hold many small items, such as a travel sewing kit, small bits of hardware for your boat (such as cotter pins), or a miniature first-aid kit. (Note: Although the materials list calls for cotton seine twine, you will notice that many of the photos show the project constructed with synthetic parachute cord. If you tie this with one more row, using 18 feet of parachute cord for accent and 80 feet of main color, you can make a neat cover for your smart phone.)

We start the tin knotted cover at the tongue (also known as the catch or latch).

Follow these steps to start the project:

1> Cut two pieces of the dark #30 cotton seine, each 6½ feet long, and middle (fold in half) each piece to create four strands.

2> Pin the four strands beside one another on the board.

The completed tin cover made out of natural fibers (top); the cover in the lower photo uses black, synthetic braided core.

3› Just below where the strands are middled, use the two outside strands to tie a square knot around the two inside strands. Use the illustration and photo as a guide.

4› To get the tongue to the necessary width, we'll add two pieces of the #30 natural-color cotton seine twine. Cut two pieces of the natural-color twine,

each 7½ feet long. Middle each one and pin them just below the knot in the dark-color twine. There are now eight strands hanging down, half of them dark and half natural color.

5› Working with the four strands on the left, use the two outside strands to tie a square knot around the two inside strands.

A square knot tied over the two middle strands.

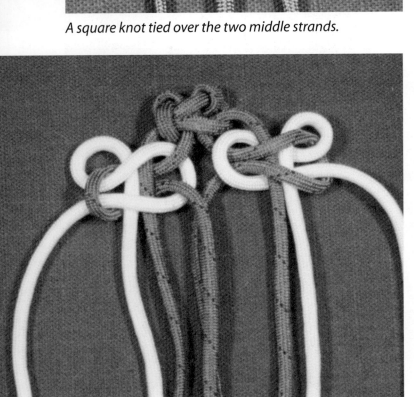

Two more square knots added to the tongue using natural-color cord.

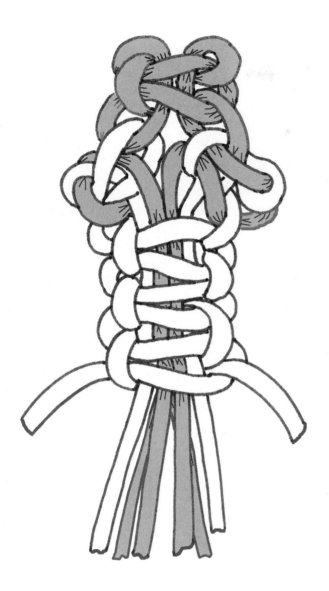

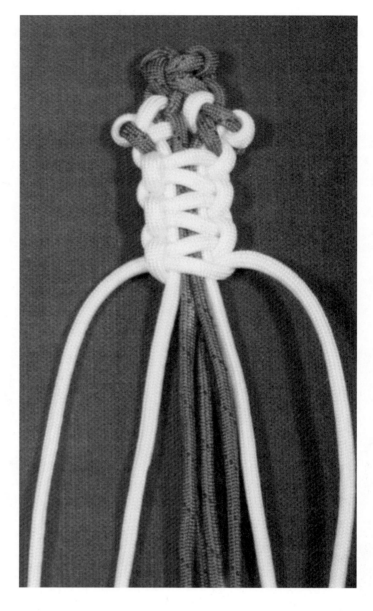

Adding square knots to lengthen the tongue.

6 > Then, working with the four strands on the right, use the two outside strands to tie a square knot around the two inside strands. Use the illustration and photo as a guide.

7 > Make sure all the slack is out of the knots. To complete the catch, use the left and right natural-color strands to tie two more square knots over the six inside strands.

With the tongue done, follow these steps to work on the main body of the project:

1 > Pull the dark-color strands off to the left and right. Then hitch each of the four natural-color strands to a pair of dark strands using a clove hitch.

2 > Tie a square knot with the four natural-color strands right under the tongue (use the two outer strands to enclose the two inner strands).

3 > Take ten lengths of 5 feet each of #30 natural cotton seine twine and middle them. Use lark's head knots to attach five lengths to the left dark-color strands and five lengths to the right dark-color

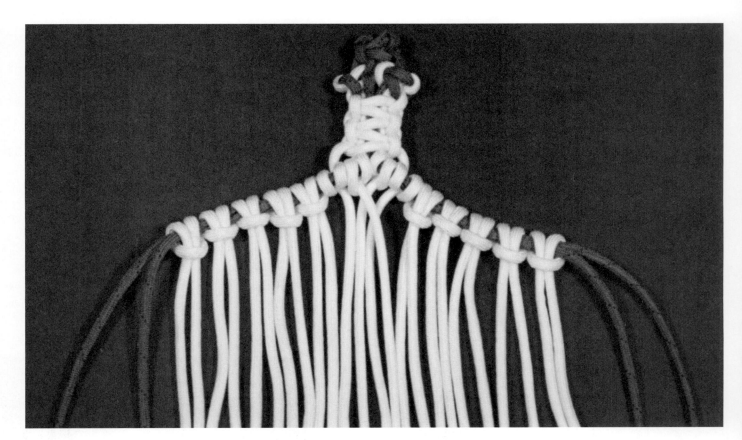

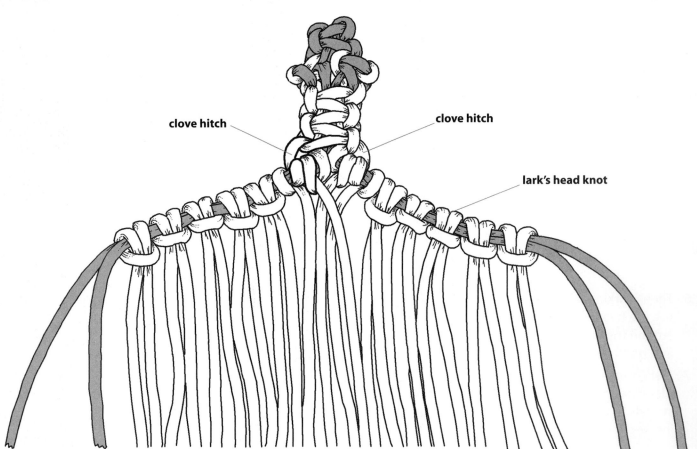

clove hitch

clove hitch

lark's head knot

Natural-color strands added to the project using lark's head knots.

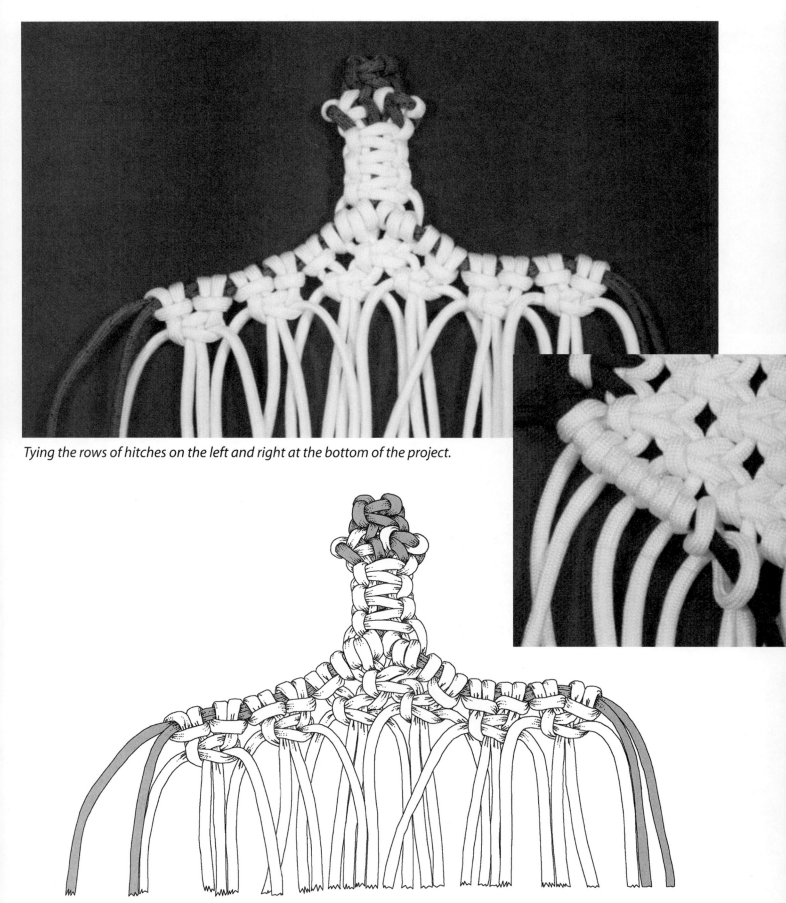

Tying the rows of hitches on the left and right at the bottom of the project.

The beginning of the process of adding square knots to create the long side of the tin cover.

strands. See the pictures for guidance.

4 > Tie a single knot at the center. To create the angled "bar" or "ridge," tie a single row of clove hitches left and right. (See the photo at left and middle of previous page.)

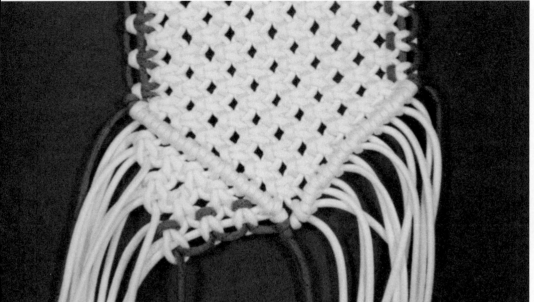

Tying rows of square knots after the hitches.

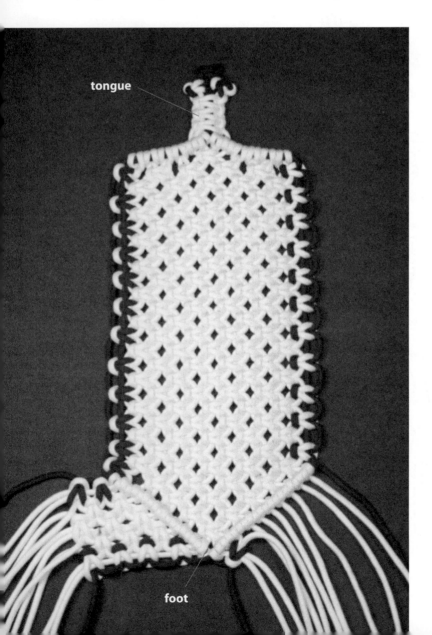

tongue

foot

The almost completed project showing the tongue and the foot.

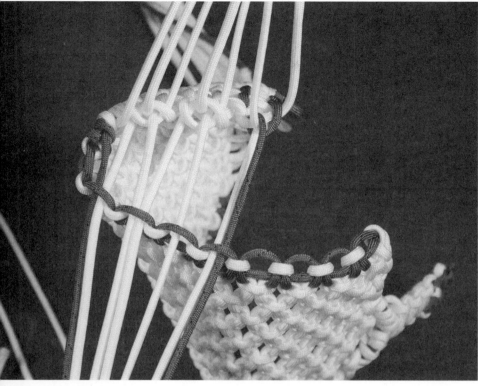

Tying off the strands to bring the cover to a folded shape that will go around the tin.

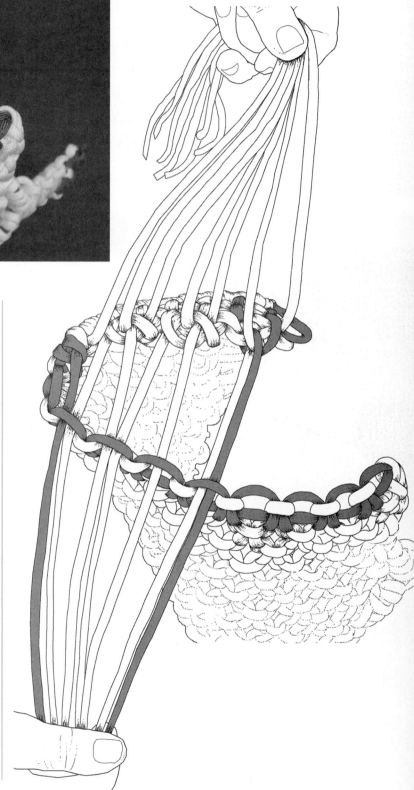

5 > For the next rows of knots, you'll need to continue tying alternating square knots for thirteen rows—that includes the single square knot at the peak (just below the tongue) and the single square knot at the foot.

6 > To bring the project to completion, we'll need to change the direction of the strands. They need to make a 90-degree turn. By tying the row of hitches right and left, we'll gain 45 degrees.

7 > To complete the turn, after the row of hitches, tie the three rows of square knots. Do this on the left and right sides of the foot.

8 > Now that the strands are pointing in the right direction, what's left is to simply tie up the sides to form the case. Do this step with the case inside out. To do this, note you have seven pairs—take one strand from each pair and thread it through the corresponding loop. (Refer back to the photos at the beginning of the project to see how the final project looks.)

9 > Pull up and tie a square knot. Put a dab of glue on the knot. (Or this can be done without the glue; I don't use glue on the cotton, but it is useful on parachute cord.) Don't cut it off too close to the knot—this is the inside of the cover, not the outside that will be in view.

CHAPTER 3 > *Projects from*

Ashley's Knot #2216

Ashley's Flat Knot #2216

In *Ashley's Book of Knots* there are about two dozen covering knots. Each is numbered. Knot #2216 is a medium-hard one to tie. I've seen it tied at the end of a tiller. The next time you are cruising around the harbor or boatyard, see how many ways you can see this knot used.

Ashley's #2216 knot.

Materials and the projects made from Ashley's Knot #2216. You can decorate a variety of cylindrical objects and balls with this knot. Note that the egg uses five leads in each bight, while the candlestick shown here uses only four leads. (The long, thin tool with the Ashley's knot at the end is a puller that I use when splicing and working on tough braiding projects.) Pigmented shellac is used to darken some of these projects.

16 feet of #48 cotton seine twine
corkboard or like material with T pins,
* or clipboard*
scissors or sharp knife
diagram of Ashley's knot #2216
superglue
shellac and brush
ruler

Ashley's knot #2216 is a wonderfully distinctive knot tied in a most unusual way.

Follow these steps to create Ashley's #2216 knot.

1> Photocopy the diagram of the knot (enlarge or reduce to fit your finger size), cut it out, and place it on a piece of board that accepts pins easily. I use a 6-inch by 6-inch piece of cork that I bought from a crafts store.

2> Use a 16-foot length of #48 cotton seine twine to create the knot. Pin the end of the twine to the diagram where the fin of the arrow is. (It will take 4 feet to go around the diagram one time.)

3> Now follow the line up a bit to where you'll see a number 1. This is where you'll want to pin your length of twine next.

4> Continue leading your cordage along the line, placing pins at each number until you reach number 16. Notice the circle at that number. The circles

Shown are the materials for tying the #2216 knot and also some of the material used for tying it around other objects (see later in this chapter).

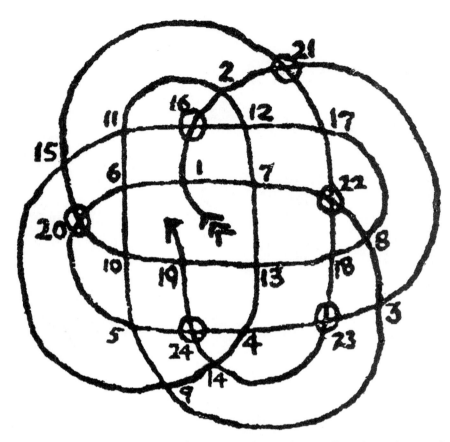

Use this diagram to create Ashley's #2216 knot. The small circles indicate where you lead the twine under the other piece of twine.

are Ashley's way of telling you to lead your twine *under* the other twine at that spot. You'll still want to pin the spot even though one length of twine passes under the other one.

5› Continue to pin the twine at each number until you finish following the diagram. You'll pass the twine under other twine at numbers 20, 21, 22, 23, and 24.

6› Now lead your end around again through the whole diagram. You'll notice that the knot is getting a little more rigid. You'll find that it's possible to remove some of the pins as you proceed around and through the mat a second time.

7› Next, lead your end around a third time. This third pass really stiffens the knot you'll find that just a pin left here and there will hold it in place.

8› Finally, lead your end around a fourth time. After the fourth pass is complete, unpin the mat. Complete the knot in your hands.

For the projects in this chapter, you need to get this knot into the shape of a cup and then closed enough to fit around a ball or other object. To do this, you'll want to start drawing out the slack in the knot. Follow these steps:

1› Hold your flat knot in the palm of your hand and use the fingers in your other hand to form your flat knot into a gently curved cup.

2› Look for extra slack in the knot. Gently pull on that part of the knot to remove that slack. Now work that slack all the way

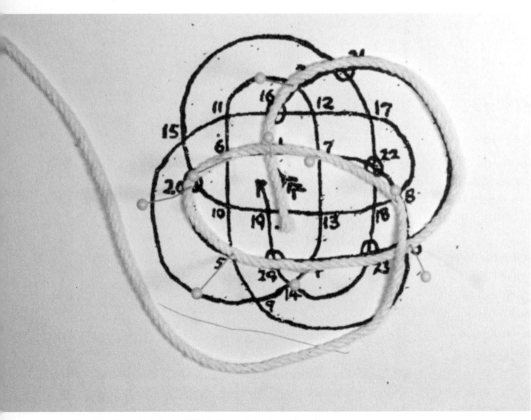

Beginning Ashley's #2216 knot using the diagram.

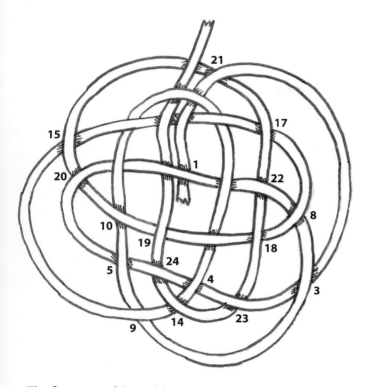

The first pass of the Ashley's #2216 knot completed.

The completed Ashley's #2216 knot.

around and eventually it will come out at one of the ends of the twine.

3> Work your way around the knot, gathering slack to release from one end of the twine. This is time-consuming work, and you'll need to go around at least three times in order to pull out all the slack.

4> As the knot becomes more sack-like, insert the ball or item you want to cover with the knot.

5> Continue to gather slack until the knot is snug around the item.

6> Use pigmented shellac to fix the knot once it is on the item.

Candlestick Holder

Add some nautical flair to a standard candlestick.

7-inch wooden candlestick holder
14 feet of #30 cotton seine twine
diagram of Ashley's #2216 knot
corkboard or like material with T pins
sharp knife or scissors
ruler
shellac and brush

Follow these steps to decorate a candlestick holder with Ashley's #2216 knot:

1> Pin the diagram of the knot to the corkboard.

2> Follow the instructions in this chapter to create the knot with 14 feet of #30 cotton seine twine.

3> Gently widen the center of the knot and slide the knot over the candlestick.

4> Draw out the slack to tighten the knot against the candlestick.

5> Cut off the ends of the twine.

6> Coat the candlestick and knot with the shellac.

Covered Wooden Egg

Here's a great gift for a young child to make with help from a grandparent to give a mom or dad.

standard wooden egg
18 feet of #30 cotton seine twine
diagram of Ashley's #2216 knot
corkboard or like material with T pins
sharp knife or scissors
ruler
shellac and brush

Follow these steps to decorate a wooden egg with Ashley's #2216 knot:

1> Pin the diagram of the knot to the corkboard.

2> Follow the instructions in this chapter to create the knot with 18 feet of #30 cotton seine twine. You'll note that the egg has five leads (strands) in each bight, so it needs more twine.

3> Place the wooden egg in the knot, and draw out the slack to tighten the knot against the egg by carefully manipulating and removing the slack until the knot encompasses or covers or coats a 2-inch ball.

4> Cut off the ends of the twine.

5> Coat the knot with the shellac.

Knob Covering

You can use Ashley's #2216 knot to spruce up knobs used at sea or ashore.

1½-inch tool knob or tiller knob
14 feet of #30 cotton seine twine
diagram of Ashley's #2216 knot
corkboard or like material with T pins
sharp knife or scissors
ruler
shellac and brush

Follow these steps to decorate a knob with Ashley's #2216 knot:

1> Pin the diagram of the knot to the corkboard.

2> Follow the instructions for the Candlestick Holder to create the knot with 14 feet of #30 cotton seine twine.

3> Place the knob in the knot and draw out the slack to tighten the knot against the knob.

4> Cut off the ends of the twine.

5> Coat the knot with the shellac.

CHAPTER 4 > *Projects from the*
Monkey's Fist

The monkey's fist is a classic sailor's knot. It often serves as a weight at the end of a heaving line, making it easier to throw the line a distance. A heaving line is a lightweight line that is tied to a heavier line and tossed from a boat to a dock or to another boat. The person on the receiving end of the heaving line then pulls the rest of the line over and ties up the boat.

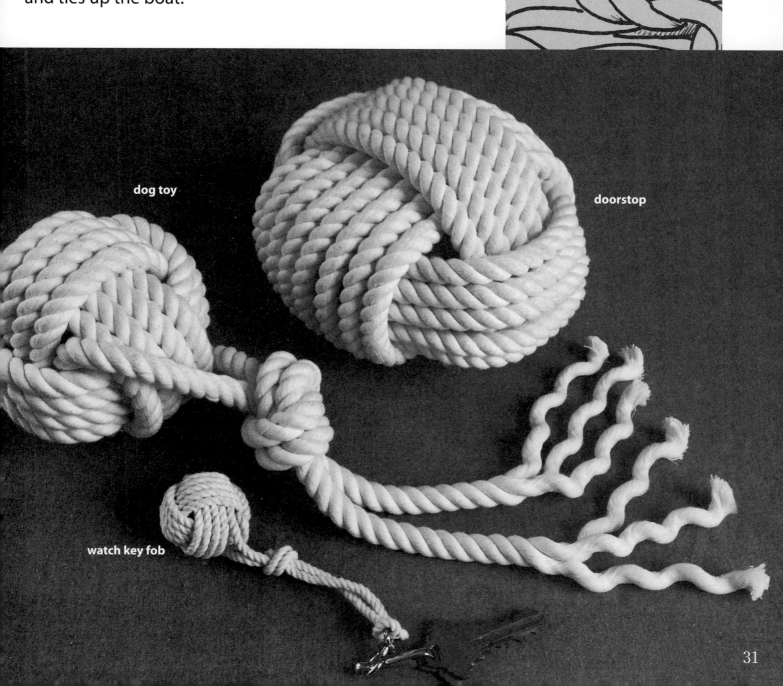

dog toy

doorstop

watch key fob

Head to the nearest beach or river to find a hefty rock for a nautical doorstop. Other projects made with the monkey's fist knot include a dog throw toy and a key fob.

Monkey's Fist

The monkey's fist knot is made by wrapping a round (or roundish) object with three wraps of cordage that are at right angles to one another. The last set of wraps goes under the first set of wraps.

Covered Stone Doorstop

For the first project we will cover a stone with ⅜-inch cotton rope (you can use manila rope if you prefer) to serve as a doorstop. (If you use a smaller rock, which is perfectly OK, then use thinner twine and a shorter length than called for in the materials list.)

> 4- to 5-inch round or oblong rock
> 16 feet of ⅜-inch cotton rope
> sharp knife or scissors
> ruler
> masking tape and/or wire garden ties (to help hold the rope in place while the knot is being tied)

The rock I'm using measures about 4 inches by 5 inches. Naturally, your rock won't be exactly the same as mine, but the mat-erials listed for this project will cover most of the rock. I say "most" because I think it

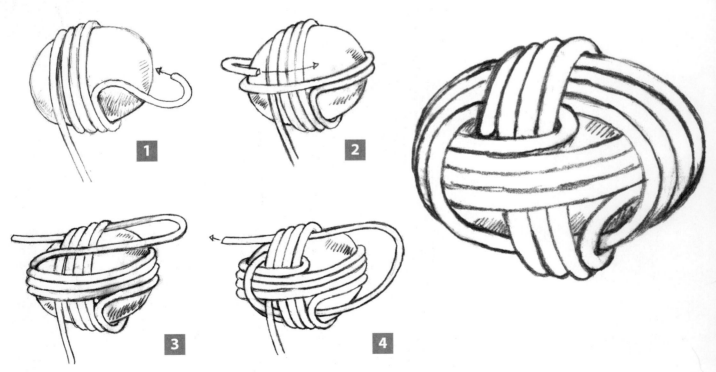

Wrapping the rope around the rock to make a monkey's fist knot.

adds a little interest if some of the rock shows.

Use the drawing and instructions below as a guide to make the doorstop.

As you make the monkey's fist knot, you might want to use masking tape and/or garden ties to hold the wraps in place on the rock. Follow these steps, which include a mock tie (steps 1 through 4) to accurately get the amount of material needed for the final tie and then a retying:

1> Take up one end of the length of rope and tape it to the rock.

2> Wrap the rope four times around the rock. As you make the wraps, leave a space between the rock and the rope about the diameter of your thumb. You will be threading the rope under these wraps later on.

3> Make a right-angle turn and wrap the rope tightly four more times.

4> Make another right-angle turn and wrap the rope four more times. Thread the rope under the first set of wraps and over

Starting the second set of wraps on the rock.

Adding the third and final set of wraps to the rock.

the second set of wraps as you add these final wraps.

5> Leave an extra 2 feet on the working end of the rope and then cut the rope.

6> Take the rope off the rock, making sure the ends are taped to prevent any unraveling. Now we'll tie the real doorstop. Tape one end to the rock and make four neat wraps around the rock, leaving a space between the rock and the cord about the diameter of your thumb.

7> Make a right-angle turn and wrap four more times. To help

The finished doorstop.

keep the wraps in line and neat, I use either a strip of masking tape or wire garden ties. Sometimes I use both because the cordage is prone to slipping off the rock.

8› This last series of wraps is the knot's finish. Make still another right-angle turn and slide the end of the rope between the rock and the first layer of wraps. Go out and over the second layer of wraps, preventing them from slipping away, then under the second half of the first set of wraps, and then over the second part of the second layer of wraps.

9› Continue wrapping until you have four passes.

10› When you have finished the knot, remove any visible tape or garden ties. Then draw out all the slack and clip the ends close. It's perfectly OK to alter the number of wraps on one or all three layers. I've done that on the larger rock shown on the chapter opening photo.

Dog Toy

This is a great dog toy. The two loose ends will turn into fringe, adding another element of interest to the dog. He or she has a choice: do I carry the toy by the ball or by the fringe?

2½-inch-diameter hard rubber ball
16 feet of ⅜-inch cotton rope
sewing needle and heavy cotton thread
sharp knife or scissors
ruler
masking tape (to help hold the rope in place while the knot is being tied)
T pins

Follow these steps to make a dog toy.

1› Unravel several inches of rope at one end. Tie off the neck of the unraveled part with a piece of cotton thread (see photo).

2› Wrap the unraveled ends around the rubber ball to cre-

ate a monkey's fist knot (see the doorstop project). Use one of the strands for each set of wraps. Use the pins to hold the knot in place on the ball as you work on it.

3› When you finish the knot, sew the neck of the rope just under the ball to keep the rope from unraveling. Sew the working ends of the strands in place under the wrap.

Watch or Key Fob

1-inch-diameter wooden ball, available in crafts stores
7 feet of #48 cotton seine twine
sewing needle and heavy cotton thread
sharp knife or scissors
ruler

The watch or key fob is an ever-so-popular novelty. Sailors around the world in all branches of service can make the monkey's fist key or watch fob. Look at the photo on the first page of this chapter to see the key fob.

The dog toy tied with a manrope knot.

The cotton seine twine I used for the monkey's fist fob shown in this chapter is #48 (6 feet in length). Follow these steps to make the watch or key fob:

1> Make a monkey's fist knot around the wooden ball. Leave 6 inches of twine free at the working end and at the bitter end of the knot.

2> When you finish the knot, hold the working end and the bitter end together and tie an overhand knot in the twine. (Note: I always sew my monkey fist key fobs because they get hard use. I wouldn't want one to come back with the ends coming out—calling into question the maker's tying abilities!)

3> As you draw up the cordage around the ball, leave the slack in one area; don't pull it all the way through the knot. You'll see that a bight of about 6 inches of slack will form halfway through the knot. It will be hanging out like a pouch. After the working ends are sewn tightly, go back to the slack and tie a tight overhand knot or a knob knot close to the ball. Now you can tie a cow hitch/lark's head knot to attach your keys.

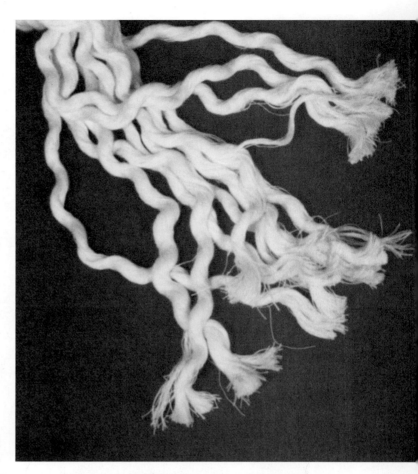

Unraveled cotton rope that makes a fringe at the end of the dog toy.

The dog toy tied with a monkey's fist around a rubber ball, finished with an overhand knot before the fringe.

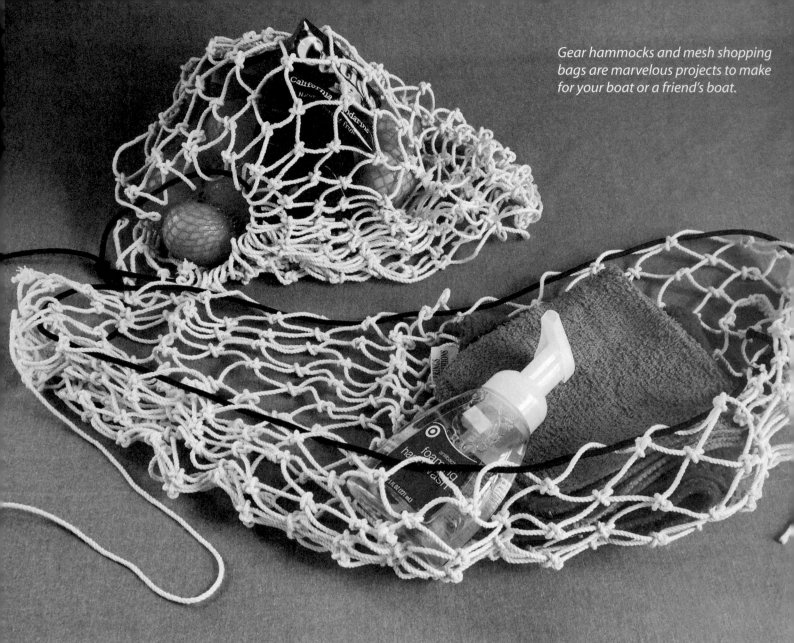

Gear hammocks and mesh shopping bags are marvelous projects to make for your boat or a friend's boat.

CHAPTER 5 > *Projects from the*
Net Knot

A net consists of a fabric of thread, twine, or cord, the intersections of which are firmly knotted so as to form meshes, or interspaces of fixed dimensions. The meshes are usually diamond shaped. It is inferred from carvings in the Cairo Museum that Egyptians used nets as early as 3000 BCE.

Net Knot String Shopping Bag and Gear Hammock

From the net knot pattern you can make two different projects, a gear hammock or a roomy string bag for shopping. A 1-pound ball of #36 cotton seine twine is enough for six items, all inexpensive, earth-friendly, useful, and fun to make.

Gear Hammock:
 12 hair elastics or rubber bands of the same size
 125 feet of #36 cotton seine twine
 5 feet of #48 or #60 cord (for rim)
 7-inch net needle
 3½-inch net gauge (also known as a spool or a mesh stick)
 2-foot curtain rod or dowel
 sharp knife or scissors
 ruler

String Shopping Bag:
 14 hair elastics or rubber bands of the same size
 125 feet of #36 cotton seine twine
 2 feet of #48 or #60 black braid (or cord) for drawstring
 7-inch net needle
 3½-inch net gauge
 2-foot curtain rod or dowel
 sharp knife or scissors
 ruler

To learn the net knot, practice tying the knot in a larger piece of cordage. You'll notice that the knot is an independent knot; it doesn't rely on another knot to hold it together, as "sweater" type of knitting does.

Examine the spaces between the knots; these spaces are referred to as "mesh." To create the spaces, we use a spool or mesh stick, which is held in place between each knot as we go across the rows.

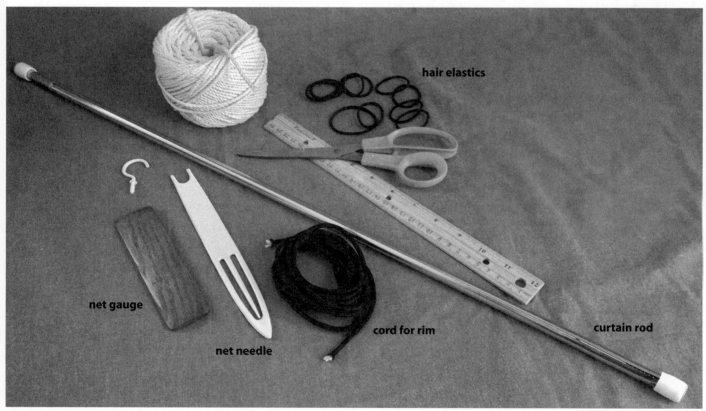

hair elastics

net gauge

net needle

cord for rim

curtain rod

The shopping net and gear hammock both use a net gauge and a net needle. The net gauge, also known as a spool or a mesh stick, is a rather short, smooth spool-shaped stick 3 to 4 inches long, usually carved from wood (or you could make one out of stiff cardboard). The circumference of the net gauge regulates the size of the mesh. A different gauge is required for each size of mesh. A net needle is a shuttle-like instrument used to carry the twine along as one works. The needle is loaded with twine (see below). If you are working on a big project, the needle is loaded multiple times, and the fisherman's knot (also known as the true-lover's knot, see Chapter 6) is used to connect lengths of twine. Net needles also come in various sizes.

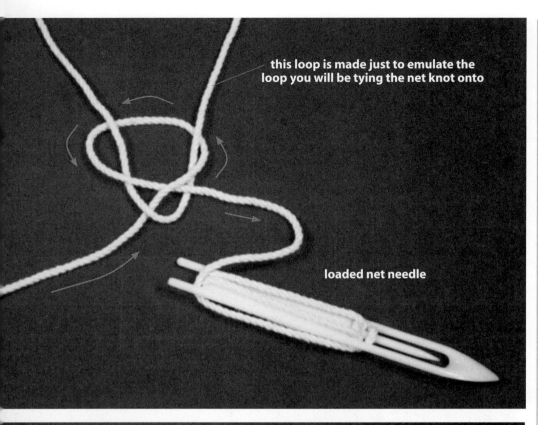

this loop is made just to emulate the loop you will be tying the net knot onto

loaded net needle

Learning the net knot (also known as the mesh knot or the sheet bend) before constructing your gear net or hammock: Take two pieces of cotton seine twine of the larger size—#60 or #48 will do. Manipulate one piece until you have a loop of about 4 inches. Bring the loaded needle up through the loop from the back going forward toward you and out. Pass it around the back of both sides of the loop, then under itself and out to the right. Snug it up tightly and there you have a net knot.

The steps to make the gear hammock and the string shopping bag are similar. Follow these steps to get started with either project:

1> Slip 12 hair elastics or rubber bands onto the curtain rod or dowel.

2> Load the net needle with 25 feet of #36 cotton seine twine. To load the needle, hold it in your left hand pointing away from you. Place the end of the cotton twine against the flat of the needle and capture it with your left thumb. Bring it up and around the tongue and then down toward the end of the needle—you'll have to move your thumb to accom-

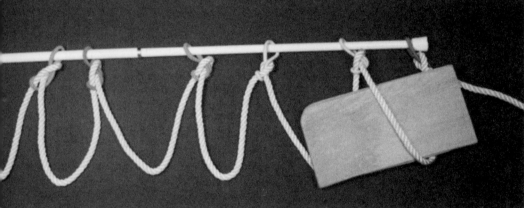

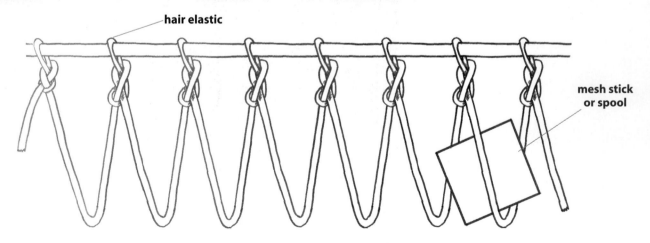

hair elastic

mesh stick or spool

Use the needle to learn to tie the net knot, then use to tie in the elastic as shown (top photos), and use the mesh stick to make sure the loops hanging down are all the same length. When done, the first row of knots will be tied to the hair elastics.

plish this—continuing down between the two prongs. Rotate the needle as you'd turn the page of a book—back and forth, not flipping end to end—bringing the twine up to the tongue, around it, and down again. Continue these steps, keeping a goodly amount of tension on the twine so the needle fills firmly.

3 > Using the net (mesh) knot, as explained in the accompanying photo and caption, follow the diagram to string the net twine to each elastic along the curtain rod. Slide the loaded needle up and out of the first elastic. Use the mesh stick to make sure the hanging loops are all the same length. Hold the stick in place with your first finger and thumb. (Remember to leave a tail of 2 feet by allowing a couple of feet to hang free to the left before the first net knot tied in the first hair elastic. This tail will be used later to gather up the head of the gear hammock.)

4 > Throw out a 2- to 3-inch loop to the left. Bring the loaded needle to the right and then to the back of the pinched pieces.

5 > Slide the needle up and out toward you through the loop you threw to the left. Pull until all the slack is out of the area and the knot is tied tightly and sitting on the top edge of the mesh stick.

6 > Remove the stick and bring it over to the next knot.

7 > Make sure you "set" or tie each knot very tightly.

Follow these steps to finish the gear hammock or string shopping bag:

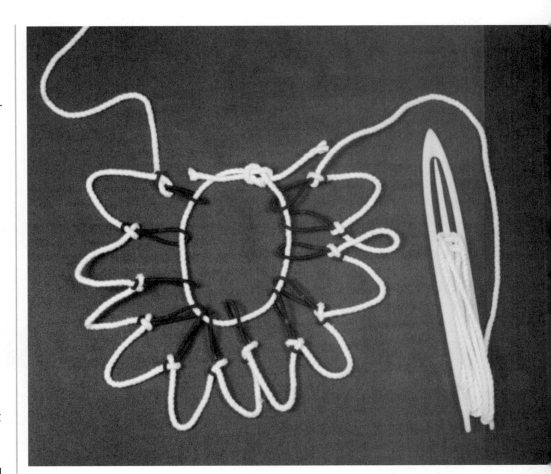

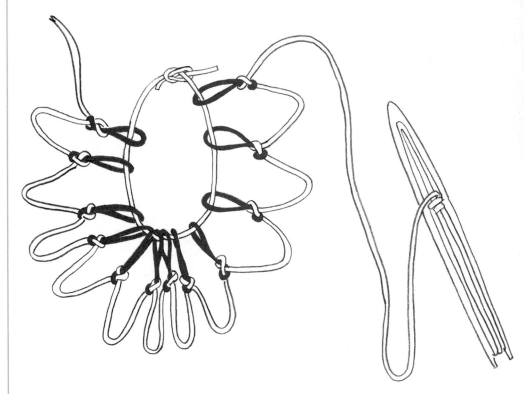

Once you have threaded the cord through the elastics (taking it off the dowel) and tied it, hang the cord on a hook and then begin the process of adding rows.

Adding length to the net by adding mesh knots (the hook holding the project is not shown).

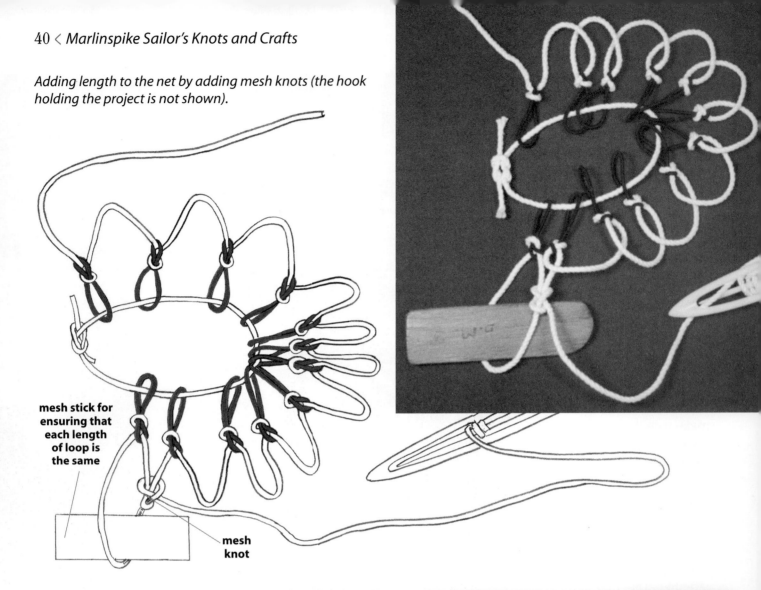

mesh stick for ensuring that each length of loop is the same

mesh knot

1> When you've reached the end of the first row, string the elastics onto a cord and remove it from the curtain rod or dowel.

2> Tie the cord into a circle about 3 inches wide.

3> Hang the cord on a hook about waist height.

4> At the end of the first row, flip your work—your row #1 will now be upside down and the last loop you 'knit' in row #1 will be the first knot in row #2.

To make the shopping bag, follow these steps:

1> Use the long tails of twine you left on the sides to sew up the sides. (There is no bottom to sew, since you are essentially folding the net in two.)

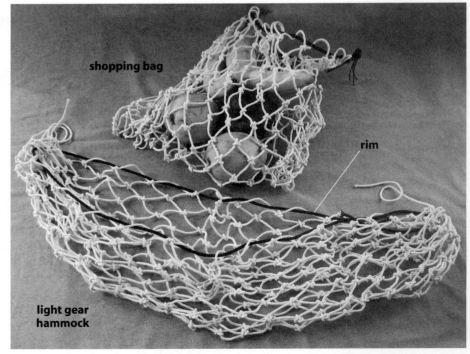

shopping bag

rim

light gear hammock

Another view of the completed net shopping bag (top) and gear hammock (bottom).

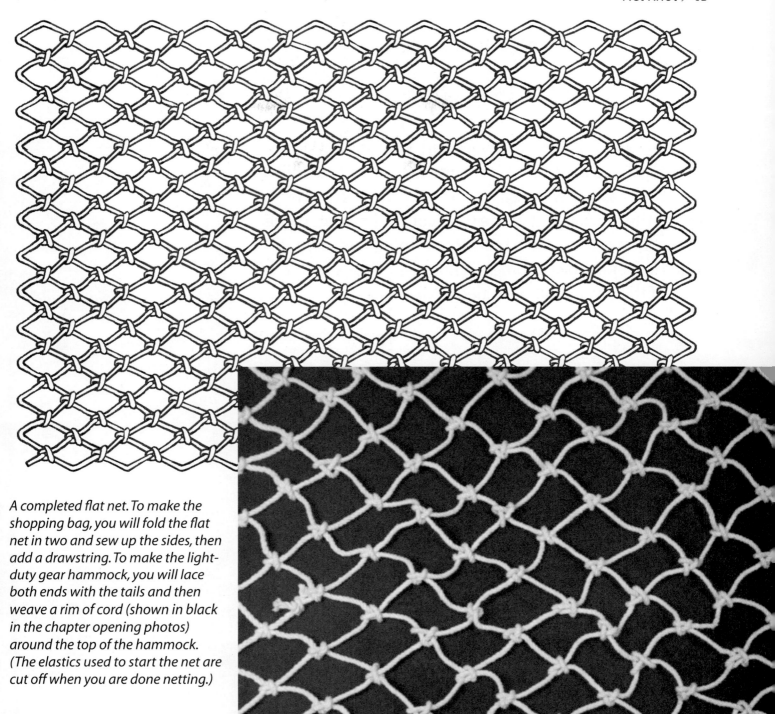

A completed flat net. To make the shopping bag, you will fold the flat net in two and sew up the sides, then add a drawstring. To make the light-duty gear hammock, you will lace both ends with the tails and then weave a rim of cord (shown in black in the chapter opening photos) around the top of the hammock. (The elastics used to start the net are cut off when you are done netting.)

2> Add a drawstring to the top of the bag. To make it easier to see the mouth of the bag, use a drawstring of a different color, such as the black cord in the materials list.

To make the gear hammock, follow these steps:

3> Lace both ends with the tail lengths of the cotton string and tie it tightly.

4> Suspend the hammock between two hooks, poles, or cabinet door pulls. Weave the contrasting-colored rim material around the rim of the hammock.

5> When the two ends of the rim material meet, gently pull on them until the hammock measures about 26 inches long. Tie the rim material together with a fisherman's knot (also known as a true-lover's knot, see page 47) and cut off the excess.

CHAPTER 6 > *Projects from the*
Carrick Bend

The carrick bend is one of my favorite knots. When tied a little loose and kept flat, this is an attractive and balanced knot. You may know the carrick bend as the Josephine Knot—the official knot of the Girl Scouts. The other name for the knot is the sailor's breastplate knot. According to John Hensel's book *Ornamental Knots*, the hoses on the front of the diver's suit were tied in this way.

A mirror frame, a decorative comb hanger, and a bottle carrier are but a few of the projects you can create once you know how to tie the carrick bend.

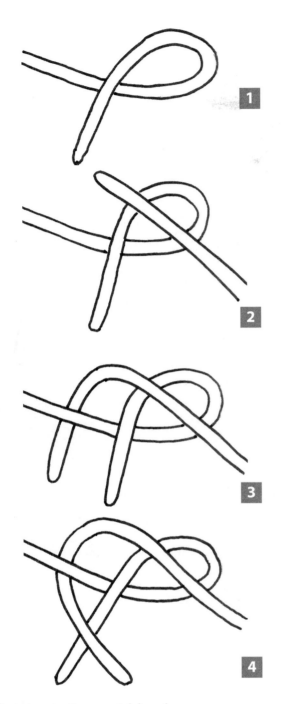

The first steps to tie a carrick bend.

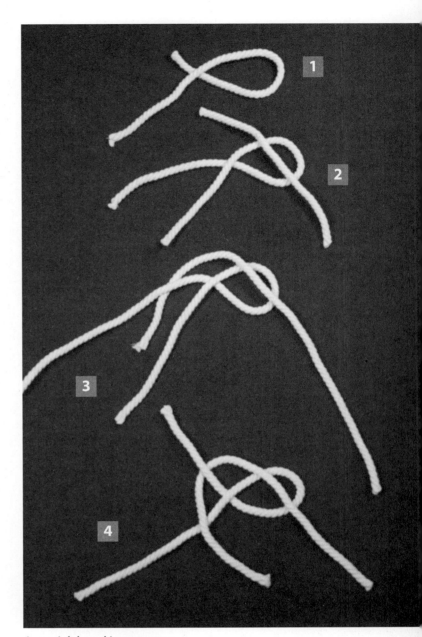

A carrick bend in progress.

The carrick bend will hold well if it is used to tie two different-diameter ropes together and then tightened.

How to Tie the Carrick Bend

For this learning project, you'll need two pieces of ¼-inch cotton rope 33 inches long.

Follow these steps to tie the basic carrick bend using two pieces of rope. Refer to the diagram for help:

1 > Make a loop with one piece of rope, with the working end lying on top (see step 1 in the illustration).
2 > Lay the second piece of rope over the loop (see step 2).
3 > Wrap the second piece of rope under first rope's bitter end and over the first rope's working end (see steps 3 and 4).
4 > Weave the second rope's working end under the first rope and over the bitter end of the second rope (see steps 5 and 6).
5 > Weave the second rope under the first rope to complete the knot (see step 7).

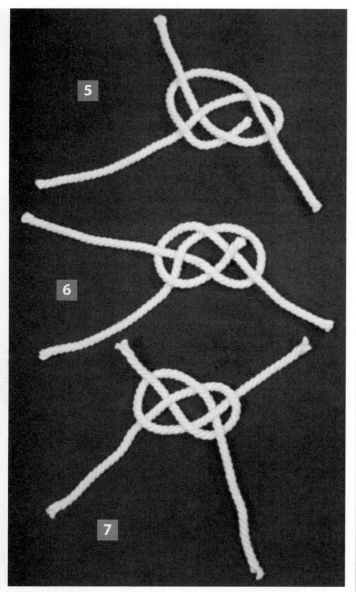

The final steps of creating the carrick bend.

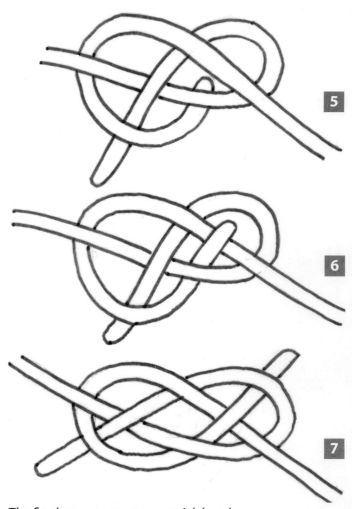

The final steps to create a carrick bend.

Carrick Bend Mirror

16-inch circular mirror
58 feet of ¼-inch cotton rope
white glue
sharp knife or scissors
ruler

To encircle the mirror pictured here (16 inches by 16 inches), you'll need a chain of 19 knots.

Follow these steps to make the knots to encircle the mirror. Use the diagram for reference:

1› Middle the rope (fold it in half) and cut it at the midpoint. Pick up the two strands and middle them again, so that you have two 29-foot strands on either side of the midpoint.

The pattern for tying the carrick bend into a chain of knots.

2> Make a loop with the two right-hand strands, laying the loop over the left-hand strands. Make sure the working end of the loop lies on top of the loop, not under it.

3> Make a loop with the left-hand strands, weaving them under and over each part of the knot to complete the loop.

4> The first knot in the chain is complete. Repeat these steps to complete more knots until the chain is the desired length for the mirror.

To attach the chain to the mirror:

1> Place the chain on the mirror, and carefully adjust the edges and check the length.

2> The ends of the bight on the last carrick bend need to be cut close and tucked in.

Six carrick bends completed in a chain.

3> Once you are happy with the fit, carefully glue the chain of knots to the mirror.

Keep in mind that everyone ties differently. I pulled every bit of slack out of the chain of knots. Someone else may tie with spaces. You might need to use more or fewer knots depending on how you tie them. Either way, the chain of knots makes an attractive border around the mirror.

ends of first and last knot in chain trimmed close and tucked in, then glued.

A completed mirror, decorated with carrick bends.

A comb hanger is a bit unusual, but you could also make this a jewelry or tie holder by tying a few thin dowels crosswise to the bottom section for hanging earrings, necklaces, or neckties.

Cotton Rope Comb Hanger or Jewelry Rack

16 feet of ¼-inch cotton rope
10 feet of #30 cotton seine twine
sharp knife or scissors
ruler

I chose this project to complement the mirror. You'll need 16 feet of ¼-inch rope and 10 feet of small stuff (#30 twine) to serve as a seizing for the tassels.

Comb hangers are unique and interesting items. They were tied on whaling ships as gifts for the sailor's mother, sweetheart, or wife. The ladies would tuck their combs in the long strands. Now, these were not the combs of today—the combs I'm referring to were ornate and highly decorated. These pieces of art were worn in the hair all day as part of the style of dress.

Follow these steps to make a comb hanger:

1 > Middle (fold in half) two pieces of ¼-inch cotton rope 4 feet long.

2 > Tie a single carrick bend with the strands (see photograph).

3 > Take the remaining 8 feet and cut it into 2-foot lengths.

The carrick bend used to make the comb hanger.

4 > Lash (or whip) each length to the four ends that exit the carrick bend using the #30 cotton seine twine.

5 > Unlay the lengths below the lashings so the comb can get a good grip on them.

Water Bottle Carrier

standard water bottle, roughly
8 to 9 inches tall and 3 inches
in diameter
45 feet of #60 cotton seine twine
sharp knife or scissors
ruler
masking tape

Here's a fun and practical project —a holder for your water bottle.

To make the base of the carrier, follow these steps:

1 > Make a circle of twine about the size of a quarter and about 1½ inches wide.

2 > Tie the circle with a fisherman's knot/true lover's knot (see steps 1 through 4 in the diagram). The advantage to this knot is that once it is tied

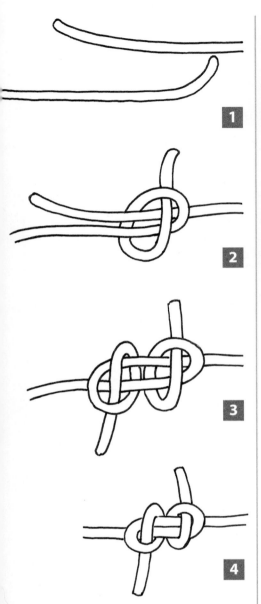

1

2

3

4

How to tie the fisherman's knot.

halfway (after you finish step 2), you can easily adjust the size.

Cut four 10-foot pieces of the #60 cotton seine twine. Middle them (fold them in half) and tie them to the circle, evenly spaced, with a lark's head knot/cow hitch (see Chapter 2 to learn how to tie a lark's head knot).

Move out a bit and tie a carrick bend in each of the four pairs of twine created by the lark's head knot (see diagram).

A water bottle carrier is a useful gift for almost anyone.

The completed fisherman's knot (also known as the true-lover's knot) shown on the right.

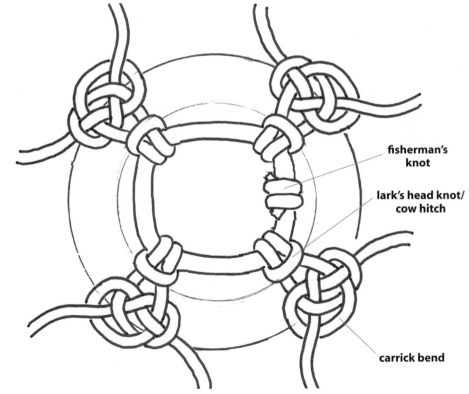

fisherman's knot

lark's head knot/ cow hitch

carrick bend

Lark's head knots and carrick bends added to the original circle of twine on the base of the water bottle that was tied with the fisherman's knot.

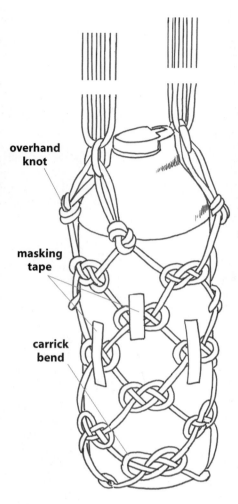

overhand
knot

masking
tape

carrick
bend

*Alternating carrick bends form a
diamond pattern on the water bottle.*

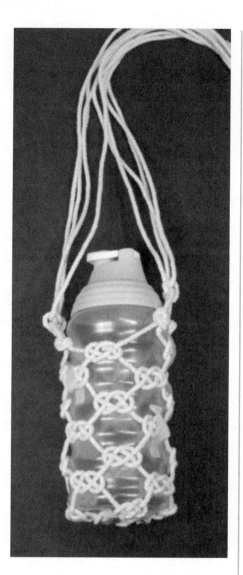

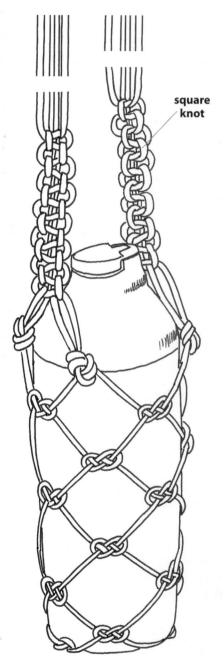

square
knot

*Square knots added to create a
handle for the water bottle holder.*

Place the water bottle on the twine base.

To make the sides and handle for the carrier, follow these steps:

1 › Pick up two strands from adjacent carrick bends and tie them into a carrick bend.

2 › Continue to tie carrick bends up the side of the bottle in alternating fashion (see diagram). You'll find that the knots slip out of place quite easily, so using bits of making tape to hold them in place on the bottle will help immensely.

3 › When you get to the top of the bottle, tie an overhand knot in each set of strands.

4 › Gather four adjacent strands together and loosely tie six square knots with them, wrapping the two outer strands around the two inner strands, to make the handle for the carrier (see Chapter 2 to learn how to tie square knots).

5 › Repeat these square knots with the other four strands (see diagram).

6 › Make a tunnel-like space down the middle of one set of the square knots. Work the loose ends from the other set of square knots through the space in the first set and out the bottom of the square knots.

7 › Repeat this process with the remaining set of loose ends.

8 › Pull on each set of loose ends to make sure all the slack is out of the center. Tie a nice overhand knot in each set to stop your work from coming apart.

Two mats made in varying lengths, with three passes each, and an eyeglass case whose backing is an ocean plat knot. The darker mat is made from manila, the lighter from sisal.

CHAPTER 7 > *Projects from the*
Ocean Plat Knot

The ocean plat knot is a variation on the carrick bend, described in Chapter 6. When the ocean plat knot is tied with ⅝-inch manila, it makes an attractive mat for the area in front of an entrance door. A version in a smaller size rope will make an excellent mat for stair treads.

Materials for doormats and other ocean plat projects range from heavy-duty manila to finer cotton twine.

To further customize your mat, add or subtract the number of times you pass the rope around while making the knot. For example, I tied the doormats out of 40 feet of ½-inch rope, with three passes. The final measurement is 18 inches by 12 inches. The stair treads are made from ⅜-inch rope, with three passes. To make either of these mats one-third larger, for example, add one-third more rope plus a few feet just for good measure.

This chapter also includes an eyeglass case project, which features a canvas backing sewn to an ocean plat knot.

Manila Doormat

40 feet of ½-inch manila rope
6 feet of #30 cotton seine twine
fid
waxed sailor's twine and sail needle
masking tape
sharp knife or scissors
ruler

To tie the ocean plat knot, see the diagram and follow these steps:

1 › Middle (fold in half) a 40-foot length of ½-inch manila rope. Tie a modified version of the carrick bend (see step 1 in the illustration on page 52).

2 › Bring the two strands up and out of the way. Draw down the two loops by pulling the slack out of the free ends (see step 2 on page 52).

3 › Flip both loops up and to the right (see step 3 on page 52).

4 › Place the right loop on top of the left loop (see step 4 on page 52).

5 › Bring the both loose strands down and weave them through the bottom of the knot exactly as shown (see step 5 on page 52).

6 › At this point the ocean plat knot is finished. To finish your three-pass doormat, you need to take the

Doormats and stair treads in both manila and cotton are shown here. Some have three passes, as in the instructions below, and some have four passes.

The carrick bend is used to tie the ocean plat knot. For a step-by-step guide to tying the carrick bend, see Chapter 6.

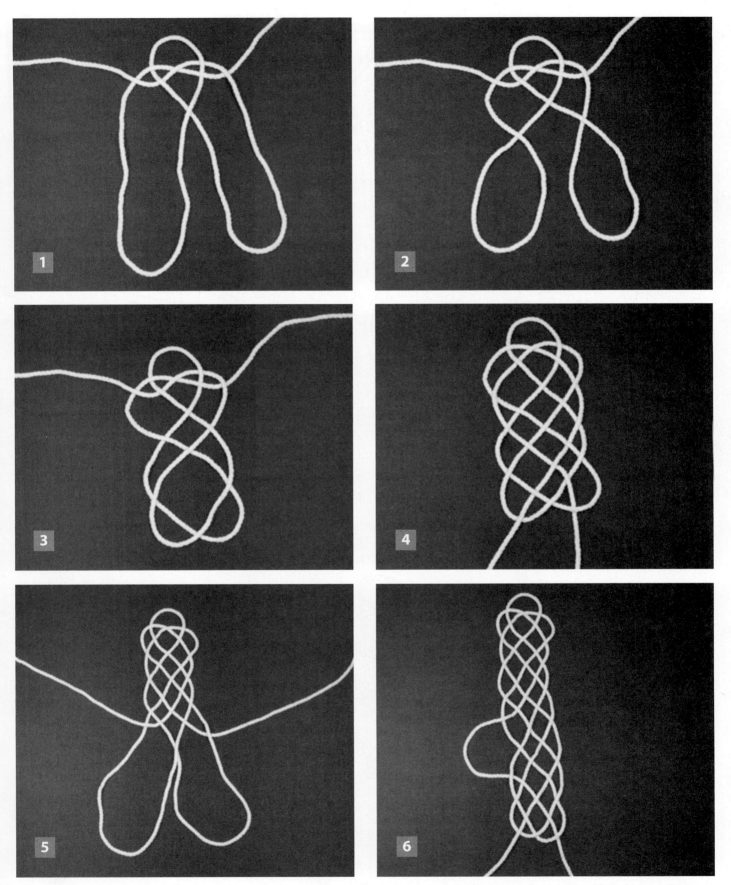

The steps in tying a cotton doormat (1 to 4) also see illustration, next page; the last two photos (5 and 6) show a doormat being tied with more bights.

The first four steps to tie the ocean plat knot (photos 1–4 on previous page match steps 2–5 here).

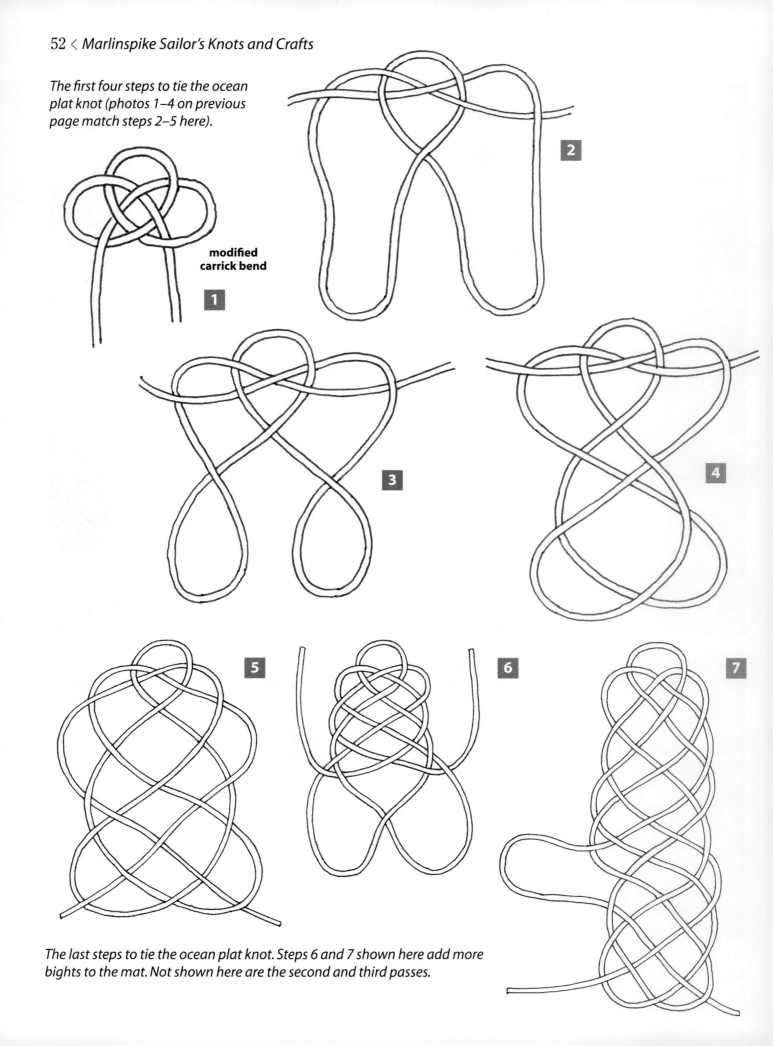

modified carrick bend

The last steps to tie the ocean plat knot. Steps 6 and 7 shown here add more bights to the mat. Not shown here are the second and third passes.

Completed ocean plat knot doormat made of cotton with four passes.

ends and pass them over and under around the knot a second and third time (see step 6 on page 52). Draw up the slack to finish the doormat.

7> Working the material up tightly can be challenging with the heavy manila—the fid may help.

8> To finish the mat, cut the ends and sew them to the underside of the mat using the waxed sailor's twine and needle.

Stair or Companionway Step Treads

48 feet of ³⁄₈-inch cotton or manila rope
#24 cotton seine twine
sharp knife
ruler

For the white stair mats that are pictured, I used 48 feet of ³⁄₈-inch cotton rope to tie an ocean plat knot. To make the mat longer, I repeated steps 2, 3, 4, and 5 from the manila doormat project. As I did in the doormat, I passed the remaining strands through the knot a second and third time.

Eyeglass Case

12-inch-square piece of canvas with embroidery
20 feet of #72 cotton seine twine
template for the project (see page 55)
pins
sewing needle and heavy thread
scissors
ruler
glue (school variety of white glue is fine)

Here's a project that encompasses the best of two elements of knot tying. Embroidery is often found on a sailor's fanciwork. Here I've embroidered a canvas

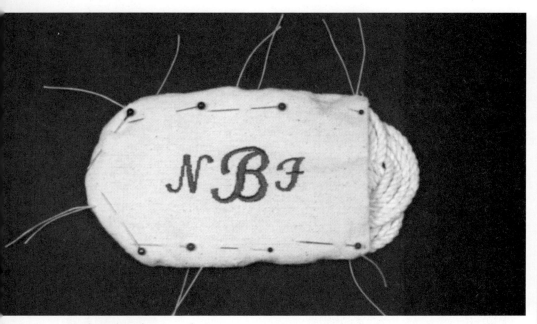

Embroidered canvas being sewn to an ocean plat knot to create an eyeglass case.

backing and sewn it to an ocean plat knot.

To make the ocean plat knot for this project, use 20 feet of #72 cotton seine twine and make four passes. When the knot is complete, sew the working ends to the bottom of the knot. The finished knot for the case shown here measures 3½ inches by 6½ inches.

The embroidery on the canvas is 1½ inches by 3 inches. It's best to embroider the canvas (or ask someone to embroider it for you) before it is cut into an oval shape.

Follow these steps to assemble the eyeglass case:

1› Using the template as a guide, cut the canvas to make the

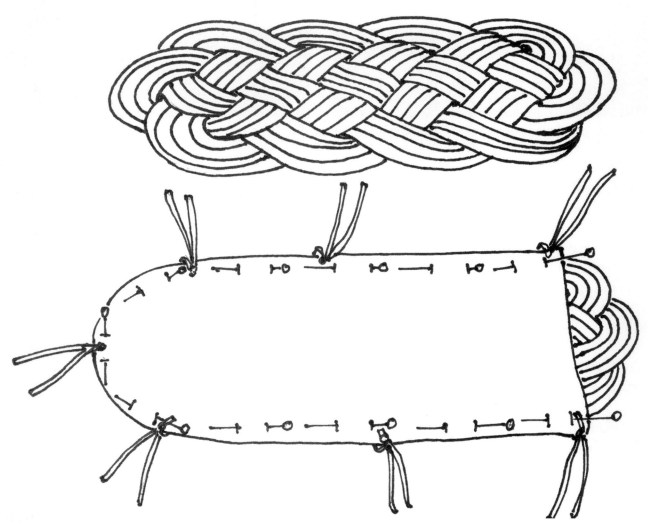

The finished ocean plat knot and an illustration of how to sew it to the canvas.

back of the eyeglass case. Cut the canvas a little wider than the knot so that there is room to fold over the hem.

2> Apply a thin coat of glue along all the edges of the canvas to prevent them from unraveling.

3> At the end where the glasses will slide in and out of the case, fold the canvas back 1½ inches (fold away from the embroidered side). Rub the fold with your fingers to set it with the glue.

4> Fold in the hem (¼ inch) under the canvas around the edge of the oval, marked with the dashed line on the template. Set the hem by rubbing it with your fingers. To keep the hem in place, pin it in a few places.

5> After the glue on the canvas dries, place your eyeglasses in between the mat knot and the embroidered canvas (with the embroidery facing outward). Use seven or eight stitches to hold the canvas in place against the ocean plat knot, adjusting the hem in or out for a perfect fit.

6> To complete the case, do a tidy running stitch around the edge to attach the back to the front permanently.

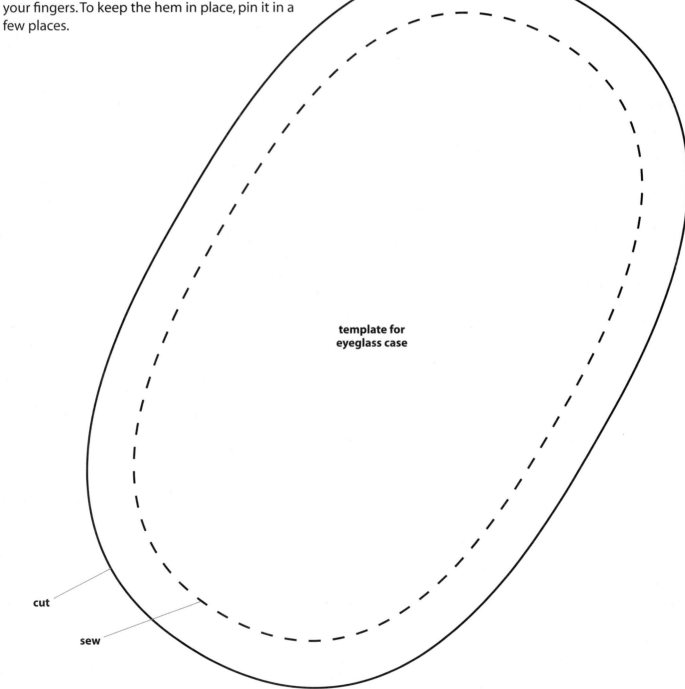

template for
eyeglass case

cut

sew

CHAPTER 8 > *Decorative Hitchings:*

Double French, Zig-Zag, Single French, and Ring Bolt

I have heard that hitching originated from the whalers who were introduced to it by South American cattle ranchers—gauchos—who tied fancy and ornate whips, bridles, and harnesses.

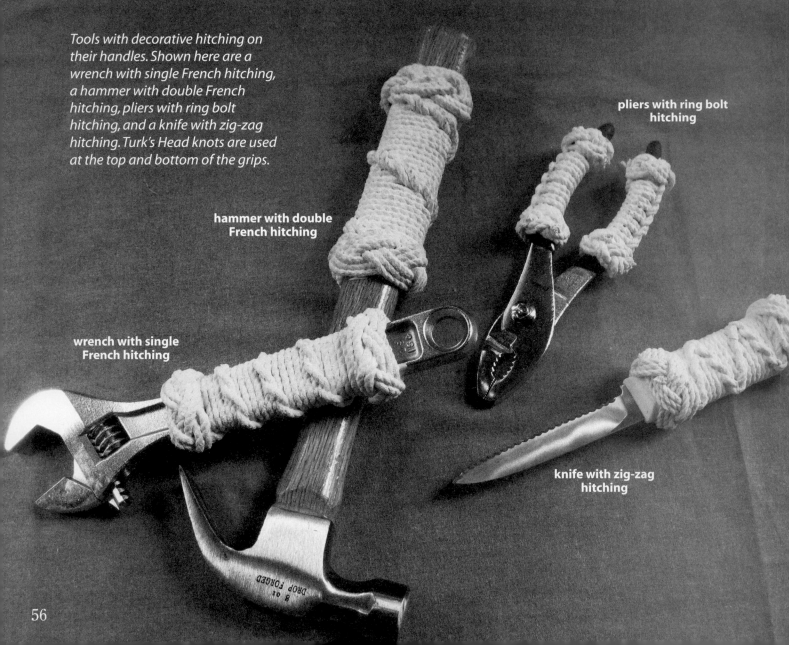

Tools with decorative hitching on their handles. Shown here are a wrench with single French hitching, a hammer with double French hitching, pliers with ring bolt hitching, and a knife with zig-zag hitching. Turk's Head knots are used at the top and bottom of the grips.

pliers with ring bolt hitching

hammer with double French hitching

wrench with single French hitching

knife with zig-zag hitching

Applying a hand-knotted covering to an object is sure to attract an admiring glance or comment. The cotton cordage used in these projects will get dirty with use (or, depending on your viewpoint, grow a wonderful "patina" with age). After the hitches are tied, I coat them with poly, shellac, paint, or resin to keep the work tight.

Once you master hitching, don't stop with tool handles. Anything in the right shape can get a decorative cover. For example, I know many sailors who cover a cigar tube with hitching as a case for needles or other small items. (The photos in this chapter show the hitches being tied onto dowels, not the actual objects.)

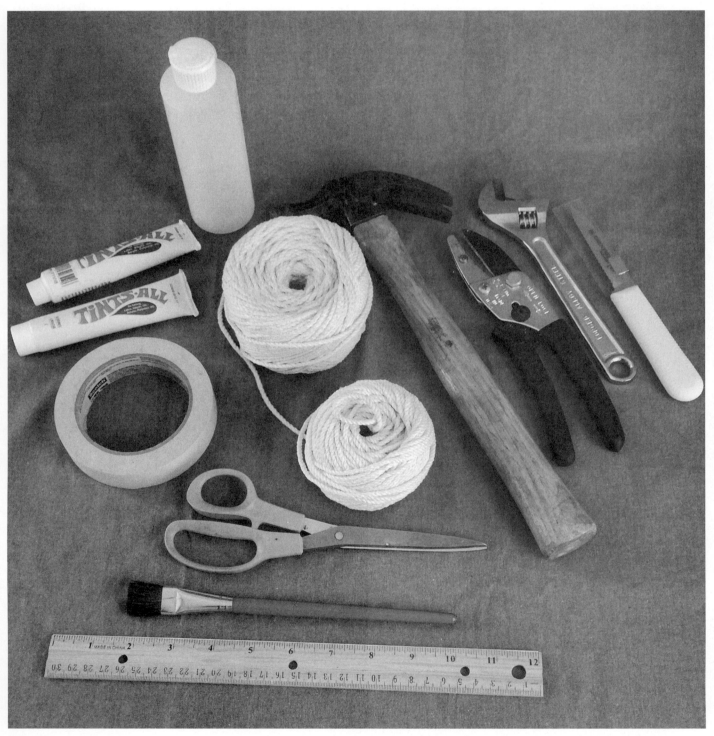

Supplies used to add hitching to tools. The tubes contain a tint that might be added to the shellac if colored hitching is desired.

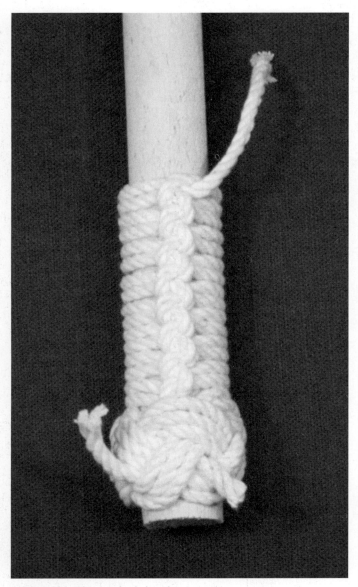

A dowel with ring bolt hitching on it.

Tool Grips

Pliers with Ring Bolt Hitching

3 feet of #36 cotton seine twine used to create the grips

3 feet of #36 cotton seine twine used to create the decorative Turk's Head knots

sharp knife or scissors

shellac with brush

ruler

To create the ring bolt hitching, follow these steps:

1> Cut 1½ feet of #36 cotton seine twine. Tie one end of the twine tightly around the top of one handle of the pliers.

2> Loop the twine around the handle as shown in the diagram, creating a straight "spine" of knots on the outside of the handle, alternating the direction left to right, then right to left, flipping the tool as described in the knife handle directions on page 61.

3> When you reach the end of the handle, just cut off the twine, leaving a 4- to 5-inch tail.

4> At the top and the bottom of the handle, use twine to create a Turk's Head knot that overlaps the end of the ring bolt hitches. Each Turk's Head knot uses 2 feet 10 inches of twine. To get the Turk's Head knot into the round shape to use at the end of the hitching, tie the knot on the flat (see Chapter 1). Then as you draw the knot up, form it around a wooden spoon handle or a fat marking pen at its center.

5> Repeat the ring bolt hitching and Turk's Head knots on the other handle of the pliers.

Ring bolt hitching in progress, with a Turk's Head knot tied at the bottom.

Wrench with Single French Hitching

8 feet of #48 cotton seine twine used to create the grip

26 inches of #48 cotton seine twine used to create the decorative Turk's Head knots

sharp knife or scissors

shellac with brush

ruler

To cover the wrench handle with single French hitching, follow these steps:

1 > Tie one end of the 8-foot length of #48 cotton seine twine tightly around the bottom of the handle.

2 > Loop the strand of twine around the handle and under the twine, as shown in the diagram, creating a spiral pattern on the outside of the handle.

3 > When you have added all the hitches you want, tie off the twine with an overhand knot or just cut off a 4- to 5-inch tail. (The overhand knot can make a lump that is hard to get the Turk's Head knot over.)

4 > Use half the twine to create a Turk's Head knot at the top of the handle and half the twine to create a Turk's Head knot at the bottom of the handle that overlaps the end of the single French hitches. To get the Turk's Head knot into the round shape to use at the end of the hitching, tie the knot on the flat (see Chapter 1), then as you draw the knot up, form it around a wooden spoon handle or a fat marking pen at its center.

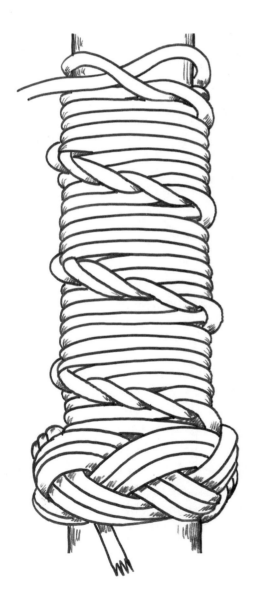

Single French hitching in progress, with a Turk's Head knot tied at the bottom.

A dowel with single French hitching on it.

A dowel with double French hitching on it.

Double French hitching in progress, with a Turk's Head knot tied at the bottom.

Hammer with Double French Hitching

12 feet of #48 cotton seine twine used to create the grip
3 feet of #48 cotton seine twine used to create the decorative Turk's Heads
sharp knife or scissors
shellac with brush
ruler

To cover the hammer handle with double French hitching, follow these steps:

1› Middle (fold in half) the 12-foot length of #36 cotton seine twine and tie one end of it tightly around the bottom of the handle.

2› Loop the strands of twine around the handle and under the twine, as shown in the diagram, creating a spiral pattern on the outside of the handle.

3› When you have added all the hitches you want, tie off the twine with an overhand knot (or just leave it cut with a 4- to 5-inch tail).

4› Use half the twine to create a Turk's Head knot at the top of the handle and half the twine to create a Turk's Head knot at the bottom of the handle that overlaps the end of the double French hitches. To get the Turk's Head knot into the round shape to use at the end of the hitching, tie the knot on the flat (see Chapter 1), then as you draw the knot up, form it around a wooden spoon handle or a fat marking pen at its center.

Knife with Zig-Zag Hitching

8 feet of #36 cotton seine twine used to create the grip

3 feet of #36 cotton seine twine used to create the decorative Turk's Head knots at the top and bottom of the handle

sharp knife or scissors

ruler

masking tape

shellac with brush

For safety's sake, before you start this project, tape over the sharp cutting edge of the knife to avoid any inadvertent cuts. To cover the knife handle with zig-zag hitching, follow these steps:

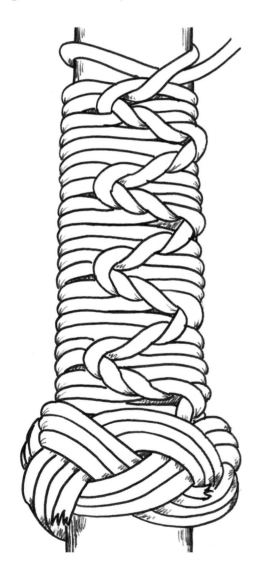

Zig-zag hitching in progress, with a Turk's Head knot tied at the bottom.

A dowel with zig-zag hitching on it.

1 > Tie one end of the 8-foot length of #36 cotton seine twine tightly around the bottom of the handle.

2 > Add three rows of single French hitching that lead to the left side of the handle.

3 > Flip the handle over and add three rows of single French hitching that lead to the left side of the handle.

4 > Flip the handle back over again and continue to add hitches in rows of three, flipping the handle over at the end of each set of three to form a zig-zag pattern of hitches.

5 > When you have added all the hitches you want, tie off the twine with an overhand knot (or just cut with an extra tail).

6› Use half the twine to create a Turk's Head knot at the top of the handle and half the twine to create a Turk's Head knot at the bottom of the handle that overlaps the end of the zig-zag hitches. To get the Turk's Head knot into the round shape to use at the end of the hitching, tie the knot on the flat (see Chapter 1), then as you draw the knot up, form it around a wooden spoon handle or a fat marking pen at its center.

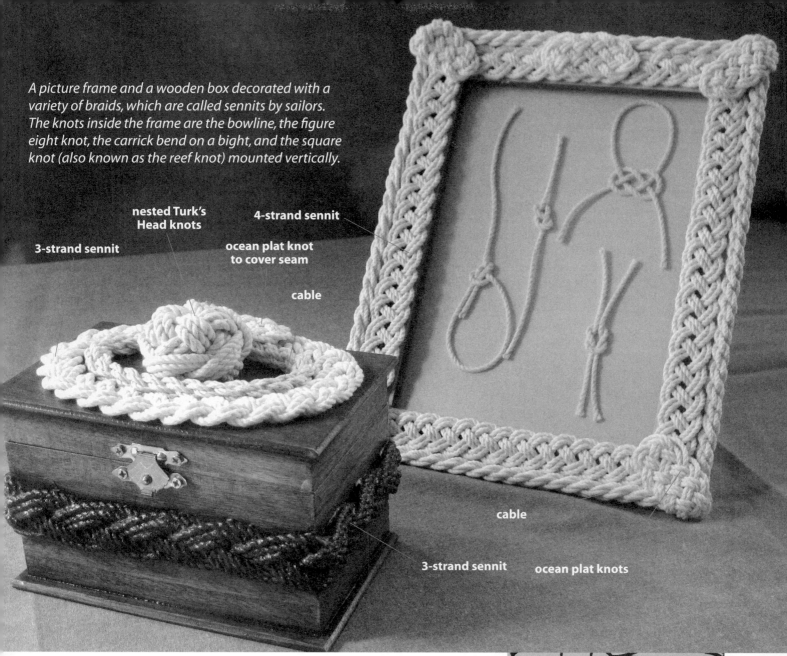

A picture frame and a wooden box decorated with a variety of braids, which are called sennits by sailors. The knots inside the frame are the bowline, the figure eight knot, the carrick bend on a bight, and the square knot (also known as the reef knot) mounted vertically.

nested Turk's
Head knots

4-strand sennit

3-strand sennit

ocean plat knot
to cover seam

cable

cable

3-strand sennit

ocean plat knots

CHAPTER 9 > *Projects from*
Various Braids (Sennits)

In this chapter you will decorate a picture frame and a wooden box with braids, known as sennits in the world of the sailor. Braids are everywhere—from ponytails on the soccer field to gold and silver braids adorning uniforms in the movie theater or the military. In this chapter you will even make your own rope to use for the decorations.

Supplies used to decorate the wooden frame and box include cotton twine and a corkboard or similar soft material to pin your work onto as you create the braids. Note, however, that our project uses a 5 x 7 frame, which holds a 4 x 6 photo (the inner black line), as shown here.

Decorated Picture Frame

5 inch by 7 inch picture frame
35 feet of #24 cotton seine twine, used for the 4-strand braid (36 inches total)
30 feet of #18 cotton seine twine, used to make the cable
12 feet of #18 cotton seine twine, used for the five ocean plat knots
white glue
corkboard or like material and T pins
masking tape
sharp knife or scissors
ruler

This small project is the perfect way to show off your knot-tying abilities. This frame displays four practical knots (the bowline, the figure eight knot, the carrick bend, and the square knot). The frame itself is decorated with the other type of knotting called "fanciwork"—elaborately tied braids and sennits.

Making or tying sennits is a lot like making a bolt of cloth. The first few feet are more often than not unusable because the cloth got started with uneven tension or the die didn't get into the cloth properly. The same goes for the end of the bolt. Mess-ups just happen. It's the same with these braids; it takes the tyer a short distance of tying before he or she finds a smooth, consistent tension to create the perfect braid. Be sure to build in a little extra braid at the end to use as a handhold. I understand that there is waste, but it's impossible to tie a perfectly smooth uniform braid down to the very bitter end.

Making Three-Strand and Four-Strand Sennits

You will use the three-strand sennit in the wooden box project and the four-strand sennit in the picture frame project.

It is fairly simple to make a three-strand sennit. Follow these steps:

1› Lay three strands of twine side by side.
2› Take a strand on the right or left and set it in the center.
3› Now take the strand from the other side and set it in the center, and so on.

The four-strand sennit is more complicated. Follow these steps and see the diagram:

1› Lay eight strands of twine side by side in pairs of two (four pairs of strands).
2› Cross the second (step 1) and fourth pairs (step 2) over the pairs of strands to the left.
3› Cross the new second pair of strands over the pair to its right (step 3).
4› Repeat this pattern to form the sennit (step 4).
5› For the picture frame, tie one long sennit, glued on the back at 8 inches, 8 inches, 6 inches, and 6 inches. Let the sennit dry, and then cut mitered corners. You will then tie an ocean plat knot and paste it over the mitered corner (see photo). Full instructions follow for completing the sennit for the picture frame.

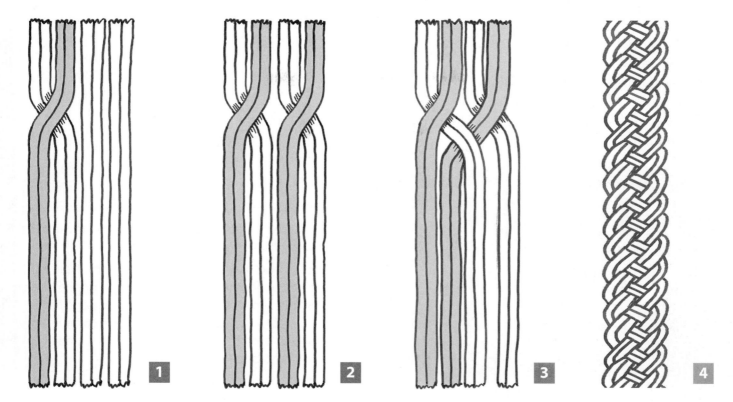

Diagram to create a four-strand sennit.

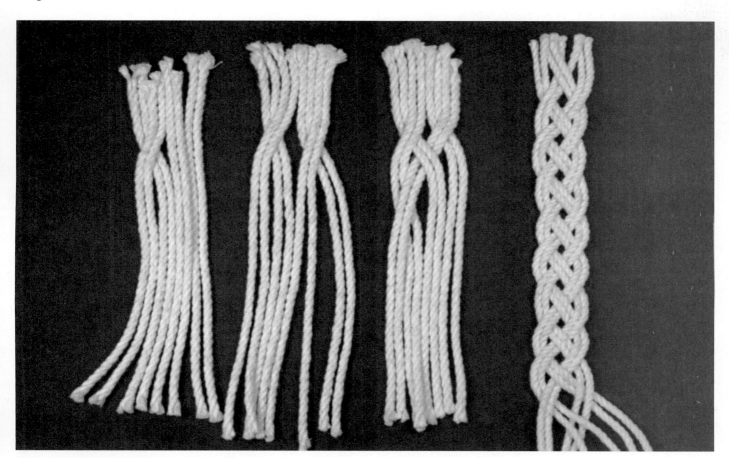

A four-strand sennit in progress.

To first tie a practice piece:

1› Cut eight lengths, each 2 feet long, of #24 cotton seine twine.

2› Tape the ends into a flat bundle and set that part into a clipboard.

3› Complete the braid following the diagram, using two strands at a time.

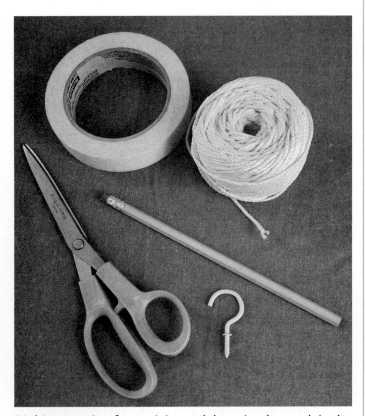

Making rope is a fun activity and doesn't take much in the way of supplies.

Making Rope (Cable) for the Picture Frame

You will use ropemaking skills to make rope to decorate the picture frame.

> *12 to 14 feet of small cordage*
> *fixed hook and pencil*
> *masking tape*
> *scissors*

To make a practice cable rope, follow these steps:

1› Cut 10 feet of #18 cotton seine twine and wrap the ends with tape to prevent unlaying.

2› Tie one end of the twine to a fixed hook. Holding the pencil horizontally about 3 feet from the hook, alternately pass the twine around the pencil and hook until you have made at least 1½ complete rounds. Tie off the unsecured end to the pencil (see photo below for reference).

3› Pull on the pencil to create a uniform tension and length on the twine. Lightly grasp the bundle of strings in the fist of your left hand with the pencil resting outside your thumb and forefinger.

4› While keeping tension on the bundle of twine with your fist, turn the pencil clockwise with the index finger of your right hand to form the cable strand (see diagram for reference). The number of twists you put into the strand will determine the firmness of the finished rope.

5› Grasp the pencil with your right hand and keep tension on the strand throughout this step. With

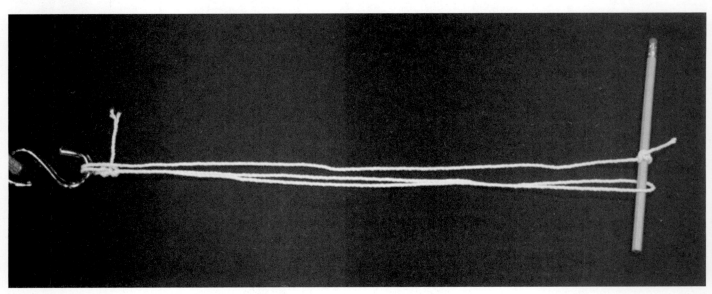

The twine wrapped around the hook and pencil.

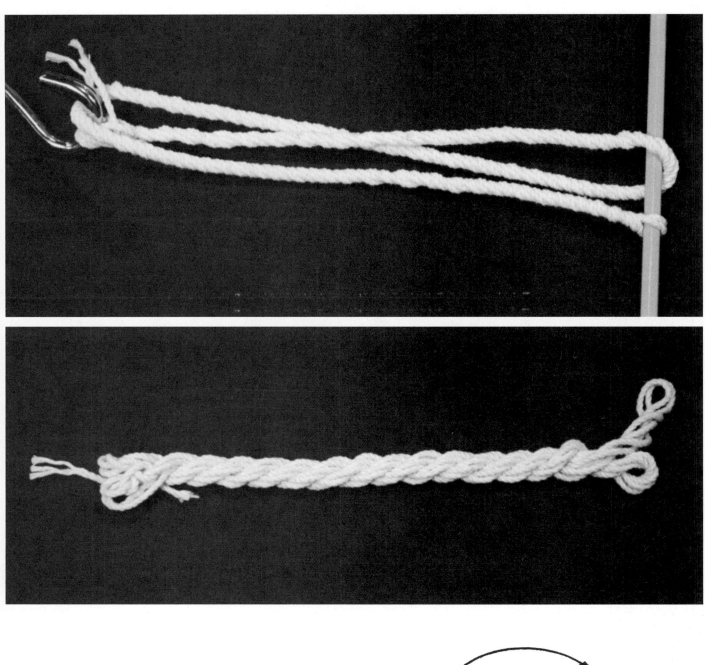

Twisting the twine clockwise to create the cable. Three variations shown.

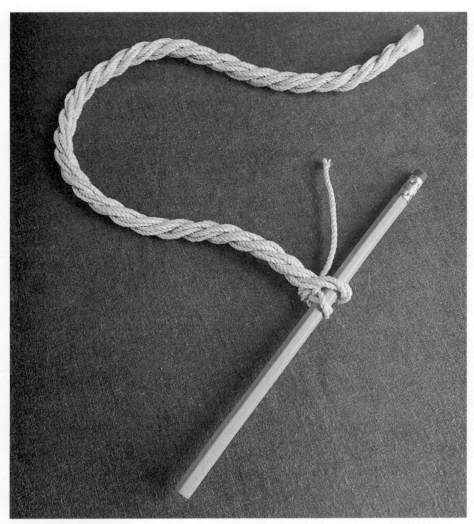

The finished length of rope, still attached to the pencil. The other end of the cable has been taped to prevent unraveling.

two fingers of your left hand, grasp the strand midway between the pencil and the hook, forming a bight (a loop). Pass the pencil behind the hook and back again, inserting it through the bight of strand in your left hand. Don't let the strands go slack. Loop the bight over the pencil.

6> Grasp the strands with your fist as before, and twist the pencil counterclockwise until it stops. The finished rope won't unlay of its own accord.

7> Tape the cable just short of each end and cut off the ends.

To make the cable to decorate the picture frame, make up one long length of the cable, and then cut it into four pieces.

Finishing the Picture Frame

The frame we're using here is a common 5 inch by 7 inch desktop frame made from wood. To decorate the frame, you need:

- The four four-strand sennits that you made
- The four pieces of cable that you cut from the rope you made
- Five ocean plat knots made with the 15 feet of #18 cotton seine twine (instructions on how to make the ocean plat knot are in Chapter 7). The braids and cables will cover the sides of the frame, and four of the ocean plat knots will cover each corner (you will center the fifth ocean plat knot at the top of the frame).

Once you have made all the sennits, cables, and ocean plat knots you need for this project, follow these steps to put the frame together:

1> To make the pieces fit together, you will need to miter the corners of the sennits and cables. To do this, apply a thin coat of white glue to the back of the sennit or cable at the lengths needed to fit the edges (approximately 8-inch and 6-inch lengths). Allow the glue to dry fully. You can then cut the sennit or cable at a 90-degree angle to create a corner without the work coming undone.

2> Glue the sennits and cables onto the frame. The diagram and picture show how to assemble the frame.

Finally, glue the ocean plat knots over the corners, and glue a decorative ocean plat knot on the top of the frame.

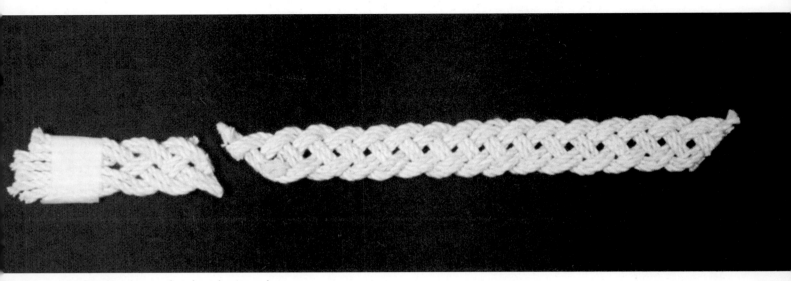

A sennit that has been glued and mitered.

Where to place the sennits, cables, and knots.

How to put together the frame. (Note: The decorative ocean plat that goes at the top center of the frame is not shown here.)

To decorate the wooden box with sennits, braids, and knots, follow these steps and refer to the picture of the box at the beginning of the chapter:

1› Create the sennits, cable, ocean plat knot, and Turk's Head knot (described in Chapter 1) referred to in the materials list.

2› Shellac the box and allow it to dry.

3› Wrap the sennit around the sides of the box as shown in the picture on the chapter opener and glue it in place. Cut its length to fit, if needed. Shellac and allow it to dry.

4› Glue the second sennit, cable, and Turk's Head knot to the top of the box as shown. Cut their length to fit, if needed.

5› Cover the "seam" where the sennit and cable meet on top of the box with the ocean plat knot; glue it in place.

6› Tie two Turk's Heads knots and nest the smaller one inside the other as described in Chapter 1. Glue it to the center of the box top.

Decorated Wooden Box

4-inch by 2-inch by 2-inch unfinished wooden box

12 feet of #30 cotton seine twine for a 3-strand sennit around the box

3 feet of #18 cotton seine twine for an ocean plat knot used to hide the sennit seam on top

9 feet of #30 cotton seine twine for a 3-strand sennit on top

6 feet of #18 cotton seine twine for a cable/homemade rope inside the sennit on top

4 feet of #30 cotton seine twine for each base and Turk's Head knot on top

white glue

sharp knife or scissors

shellac and brush

ruler

masking tape

CHAPTER 10 > *Projects from the*
Chinese Button Knot

As a decorative knot, the Chinese button knot is right on par with the Turk's Head knot. *Ashley's Book of Knots* calls the Chinese button knot every name in the book: #787, the sailor's knife lanyard knot, the marlinspike lanyard knot, the single-strand diamond knot, the two-strand diamond knot, and the bosun's whistle knot. The *Encyclopedia of Knots and Fancy Rope Work* calls the Chinese button knot #190, the two-strand carrick diamond knot. Kim Sang Lan, in her beautiful book *Knot Craft*, calls it a lotus knot, or the button knot.

zipper pull made
of leather lace

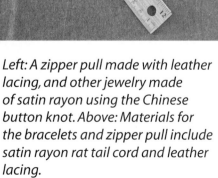

Left: A zipper pull made with leather lacing, and other jewelry made of satin rayon using the Chinese button knot. Above: Materials for the bracelets and zipper pull include satin rayon rat tail cord and leather lacing.

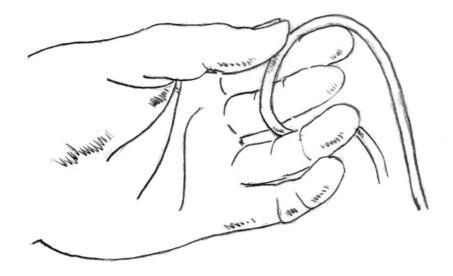

Holding the lace to start the knot.

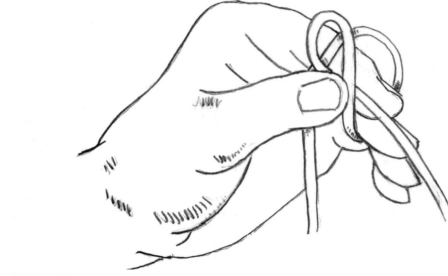

Adding a loop to the knot.

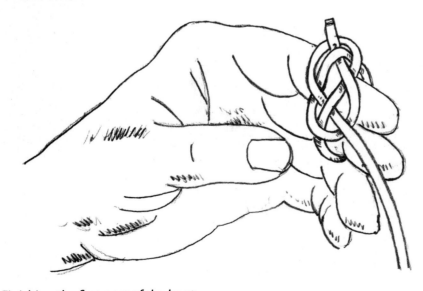

Finishing the first part of the knot.

The leather lacing used here can be purchased at Tandy Leather or at big-box crafts stores.

Chinese Button Knot Zipper Pull

two 18-inch lengths of leather lacing in different colors (the lacing is sold in packets of ⅛ inch by 8 yards)
sharp knife or scissors

A number of years ago a counselor from the local high school approached me looking for a knot that was inexpensive and easy to tie, and could be done in two colors (the school colors, of course!). I came up with the zipper pull. The instructions are below. (When the pull is completed, you can add it to the zipper with a lark's head/cow hitch knot.)

Follow these steps to make a knot out of the first length of lace:

1› Chose your first color in an 18-inch length. We're going to tie this knot around two fingers.

2› Find the center of the lace and wrap it around the index finger and middle finger of your left hand. Arrange the two working ends of the lace so that the end on the bottom leads away, and the end on the top leads toward you, as shown.

3› Bring the back lace to the front, make a twist in it, and set the small loop (the result of the twist) over the top lace, as shown.

4› Twist the left lace into a loop, weaving it over, under, over, under, and over the other laces. This knot is called the sailor's breast plate (see illustration).

5› Next, bring the bottom lace around the tip of your index

finger and through the center of the knot from behind, as shown.

6> Repeat this move with the other strand. Pick up the other strand and loop it down and through the center of the knot from behind. Now the two strand ends should be next to each other in the center, as shown.

7> Draw up the slack in the knot.

Follow these steps to add a second lace to the knot:

1> Take the second colored lace (18 inches long) and arrange the two ends so that they exit at both sides of the already tied Chinese button knot. Position the knot so that the loop is pointing down and the two strand ends are pointing up.

2> Push the ends of the first knot out of the way. Arrange your fingers exactly as you did with the first knot and set them smack dab on top of the first knot.

3> Now tie the second knot with the second colored lace exactly as you did the first one, but don't draw up all the slack when you finish the second knot.

4> Maneuver the two working ends from the first knot you tied through the center of the second knot. The working ends from the first and second knots will make a four-strand fringe.

5> Trim the four working ends to make them even.

Completed zipper pulls made out of various small colored cordage or cord.

Adding another loop to the knot.

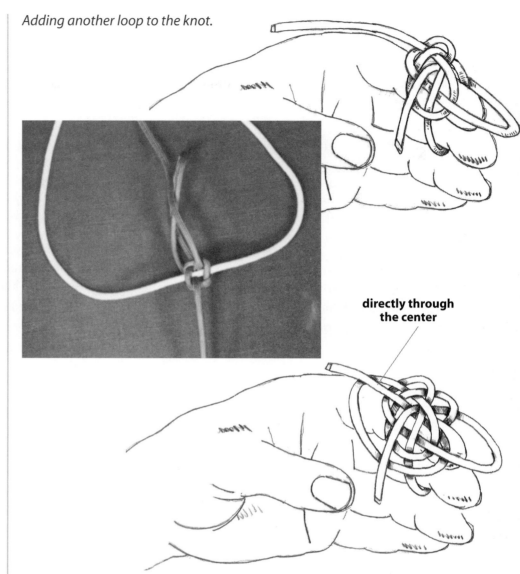

directly through the center

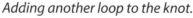

Adding another loop to the knot.

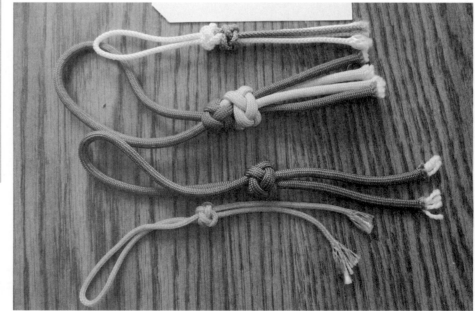

Chinese Button Knot Bracelet

72 inches of 1mm rayon pettit #0 orange cord—
or any colors you choose (it can also be made
with leather lacing)
sharp knife or scissors
ruler

As I write this book, it's summertime. The colors of the day reflect that. So for the bracelet I chose a yummy sherbet orange rayon cord. This material is available online or from big-box stores. I also tied one in black (see the photograph at the start of this chapter to see the completed bracelets).

As you'll notice I tied a succession of knots in one color for the bracelet. You can also make a bracelet or wristlet with fewer knots, spaced out farther. In the 7 ½-inch bracelet here, I tied sixteen knots in black and seventeen knots in orange.

Follow these steps to make a bracelet out of Chinese button knots:

1› Middle the cord (fold it in half).

2› Wrap the middled cord around your fingers and make one Chinese button knot.

3› Adjust the loop down to a scant half inch, then add the remaining Chinese button knots—sixteen or seventeen knots work nicely and make a 7½-inch bracelet.

4› When you finish the last knot, cut the cord close.

Chinese Button Knot Necklace

20 feet of satin rayon rat tail cord
sharp knife or scissors
ruler

Follow these steps to make an 18-inch choker out of Chinese button knots:

1› Middle (fold in half) the 20 feet of satin rayon rat tail cord.

2› Wrap the middled cord around your fingers and make a series of Chinese button knots.

3› When you finish the last knot, put the loop in front of the first knot above the last knot you tied to clasp it shut.

Wall and crown garment buttons tied with leather lacing and cotton seine twine.

CHAPTER 11 >

Garment Buttons Using the Wall and Crown Knots

In addition to the Chinese button knot (described in Chapter 10), there is another useful button made from a wall knot and a crown knot. The wall and crown is a versatile knot. Tied with a certain number of strands and manipulated just so, *voila*—a rope fender. Tied with a certain number of strands and manipulated just so, *voila*—a knob at the end of a rope railing or at the bottom of a rope ladder. Tied in a different configuration with a different number of strands, *voila*—garment buttons perfect for a blazer (if they're tied in leather) and so classy if they're tied in cotton seine twine for a fisherman's knit sweater. The garment button is attached to the garment by means of the small bight we sewed in at the start with the length of #18 cotton seine twine (the single strand). The dark-colored button shown is made from ⅜-inch leather lacing; the light-colored button is made from #72 cotton seine twine.

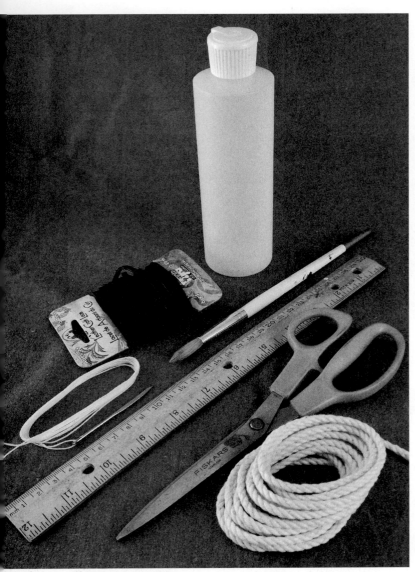

Materials for making garment buttons include cotton twine, leather lacing, a needle, and fine cotton twine for sewing the small bight in the attachment loop.

You can use these buttons to fasten garments or to decorate other projects.

Wall and Crown Garment Buttons

12 inches of #72 cotton seine twine for cotton buttons

two 10-inch-long pieces of 1/8-inch leather lace for black leather buttons

sewing needle and heavy cotton thread (#18)

sharp knife or scissors

ruler

shellac and brush

Follow these steps to make the garment buttons out of the #72 cotton seine twine. This is a six-strand wall and crown button. Directions for making buttons out of the leather lace follow the directions for making buttons out of cotton seine twine. (To illustrate this knot, we used cotton rope, and the sizing in the picture and drawing is of #18 cotton seine twine. For your button in #72 cotton seine twine, you'll want to use a single strand of the #18 cotton seine twine or a length of thread.)

1> Middle (fold in half) a 10-inch piece of #72 cotton seine twine.

2> Tie a small loop at one end of the heavy cotton thread, and thread the needle on the other end. Tie it on, seizing ½ inch up from the bight (loop) that you made in the #72 cotton seine twine. You now have a small loop bound by seizing with two lengths of twine below the seizing (see illustration).

3> Unlay (untwist) the two lengths of twine all the way up to the seizing to create six strands.

4> Tie a six-strand wall knot. Follow these steps:

5> Lay out the six strands parallel to one another.

6> Loop the left strand down in the direction the rope twists and up under the far right strand.

7> Loop the next strand on the left under and over the first loop.

8> Continue to loop each strand under and over the previous loops until you have looped all six strands.

9> Tighten the knot.

To finish this button, tie a single "topper" of a crown knot with the six strands in pairs. Follow these steps:

1> Lay out the six strands parallel to one another.

2> Loop one pair of strands on the left up and over the pair of far right strands.

3> Loop the next set of strands on the left over and under the first loop.

4> Loop the third set of strands over and under the second loop.

5> Tighten the knot.

You can use a mixture of wall and crown knots to design your own buttons. For example, the larger of the two light-colored buttons in the photograph at the start of this chapter is composed of a base of two rows of wall knots and a topper of a three-paired crown knot. It's possible to make the button even larger by adding another layer of single wall knots and another topper of a three-paired crown knot.

For the dark-colored leather button, I seized two lengths of lacing together and formed the small button with a base of wall knots and a "topper" of a four-strand single crown knot. For the larger leather button, I added to the pattern a single layer of wall knots and a topper of single-strand crown knots.

After you are satisfied with the shape and size of the button, cut the ends off closely and dip them into the shellac. This will prevent the ends from coming untied. After the shellac is thoroughly dry, you might want to paint the button a different color.

Twine middled and bound with thread (seized) to create a loop on top.

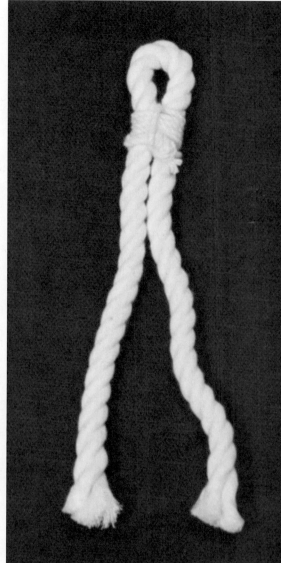

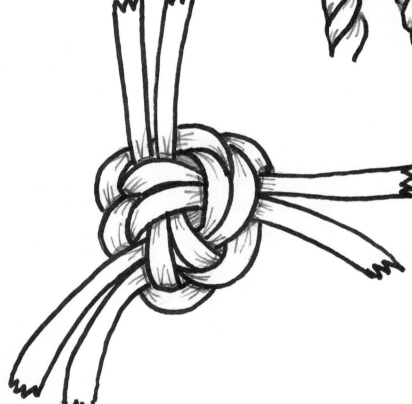

Finishing the knot with the crown.

The wall and crown knot in progress.

CHAPTER 12 >

Games to Make and Play:

Canvas Bag for Jacks or Marbles, Chess or Checkers Board, Manila Ring Toss

What better projects to make, and to engage you and your family or friends in hours of game-playing fun. Make these to use for yourself or for holiday giving.

A simple canvas bag and manila rings are easy to craft.

Canvas Bag for Jacks or Marbles

12-inch-square piece of canvas
cutting template for bag
sewing needle and heavy cotton
*   thread*
2 feet or more of #60 cotton
*   cord for drawstring*
sharp knife or scissors
four each of ¼-inch grommets
grommet-inserting tool
*   (optional)*
white glue (optional)

Follow these steps to make the canvas bag:

1 > Cut out the two canvas pieces by using the template provided on the following page.

2 > After you've cut the pieces of canvas, you might want to apply a thin coat of white glue along the top edge and both side edges of the canvas, stopping 5 inches from the bottom. This small step will prevent the canvas from unraveling as you work through your project.

3 > When the glue is dry, pencil in a sewing line ¼ inch along the sides and bottom (see template).

4 > With the outside of the canvas pieces together, sew the two halves together; don't sew the top closed.

5 > Turn the pouch right side out.

6 > Turn down the top for the hem.

7 > Insert the four grommets, two on each side.

8 > Lace the drawstring.

9 > Fringe the top hem ½ inch and embellish with colored floss or fabric paint.

With a small investment in manila and canvas, you can create hours of game-playing fun.

A finished pouch used to store marbles, jacks, or chess or checker pieces.

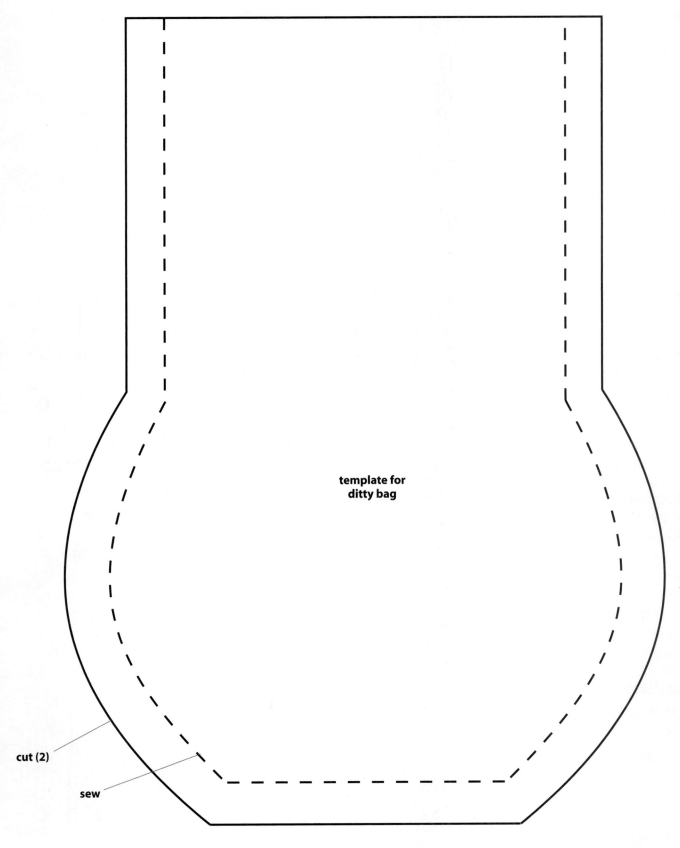

template for ditty bag

cut (2)

sew

You will cut two pieces of canvas for the bag, using this template to get the correct shape and size. Pencil in the dotted line, which is the sewing line, on the canvas after you have run a bead of glue along the sides and bottom.

Chess or Checkers Board

*piece of cotton duck canvas
10 inches wide and 2 feet 10
inches long*
1 pint gesso
masking tape, 1 inch wide
*Acrylic paint in burnt umber,
white, and iridescent bronze
to paint the board*
clear polyurethane
brushes

A canvas chess or checkers board is lightweight and easy to store. You can make a matching canvas bag to hold the game pieces.

Follow these steps to make the board:

1› Pull out 9 inches of horizontal (weft) threads from each of the long ends of the canvas to make the fringe.

Pulling out the weft threads to create a fringe.

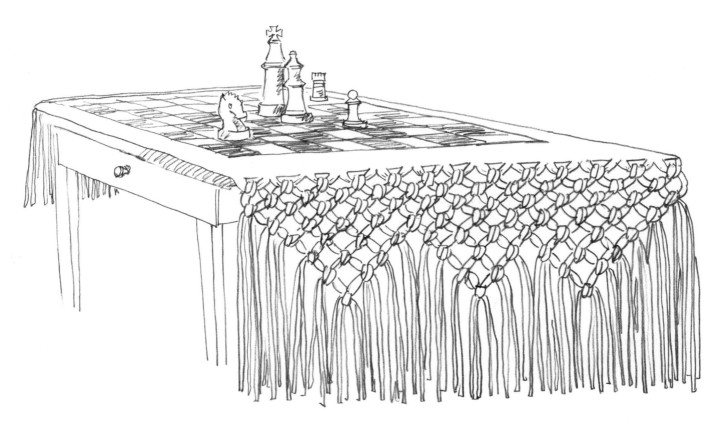

Completed chess board, with fringe hanging over the table.

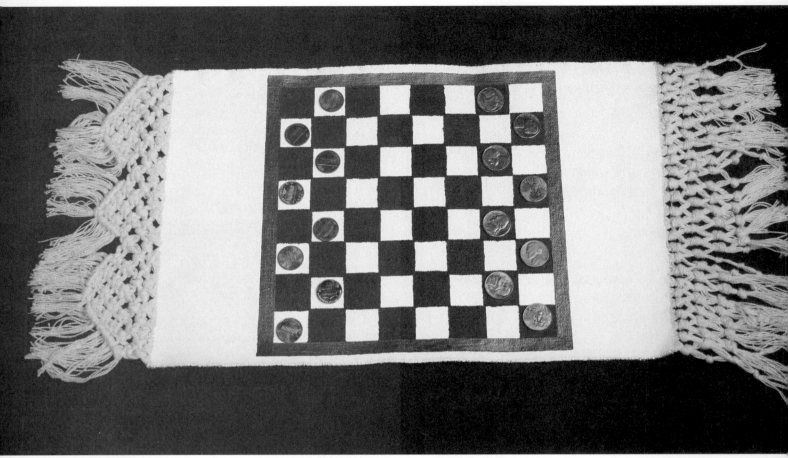

A completed canvas board.

2› Apply two coats of gesso to the canvas. Let each coat dry, and lightly sand between the coats.

3› After the gesso dries, use the masking tape to outline where the dark squares will go on the board.

4› Paint in the dark square with the burnt umber paint.

5› After the paint dries, use the masking tape to make a ½-inch outline for the edge of the board.

6› Paint the edge of the board with the iridescent bronze paint.

7› After the paint dries, cover the playing area with the clear polyurethane.

8› Add decorative knotting to the fringe at either end of the board. This fringe treatment uses a technique that goes by many names—macramé, drawn fringe lace, McNamara's lace, or even square knotting. We use square knots to make the decorative knotting (described in Chapters 2 and 7) on one end and alternating overhand knots on the other end (see illustration).

Manila Ring Toss

7 feet of ⅝-inch manila rope
sewing needle and heavy cotton thread
sharp knife
ruler
masking tape

The rings we're making here will serve very well as an option for the kids or more gentle folk for the next game of horseshoes you attend this summer. The material of choice here is three-strand ⅝-inch manila rope. These rings also work well as a pair of handles on a wooden chest.

Follow these steps to make a manila ring:

1› Unlay (unwind the strands in) the 7 feet of ⅝-inch manila, taking care to preserve the twist in the rope. You now have three strands of rope. Tape the end of each strand to prevent unraveling.

2› Lay one strand full length on a table. Leaving a tail of 18 inches to the right, form a circle about 6 inches in diameter going in a counterclockwise direction (see diagram). The longest tail will be on the left side of the circle.

3> Next, wrap the tail on the right in a clockwise spiral around the circle. Because we've taken care to preserve the natural lay and twist of the rope, the strand will find its way into the right spot. Look at the diagram for guidance, and use a gentle hand to coax the strand to lay just right.

4> Wrap the tail on the left counterclockwise around the circle. Again, go easy with the pressure; the strand will want to fall into just the right spot.

Completed manila rings ready for a game.

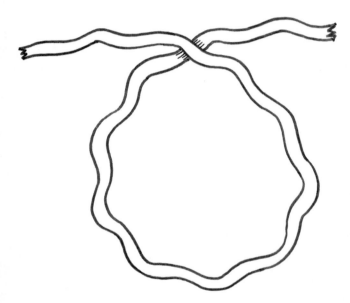

Forming the circle for the grommet.

The circle in manila used to make the grommet.

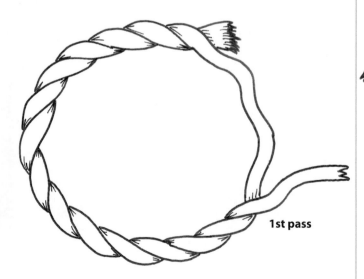

Wrapping the tail clockwise around the circle.

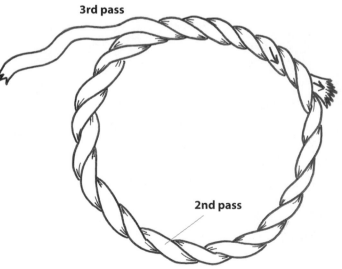

Wrapping the left tail counterclockwise around the circle.

5› To complete the job, carefully cut off the ends of the tails you wrapped clockwise and counterclockwise so that they butt up each other.

6› Now apply a 1-inch-wide tight whipping with the heavy cotton thread (see diagram).

7› Continue making rings until you have enough for your game.

The left tail being wrapped around the circle.

The finished ring.

Whipping added to the ring to finish it.

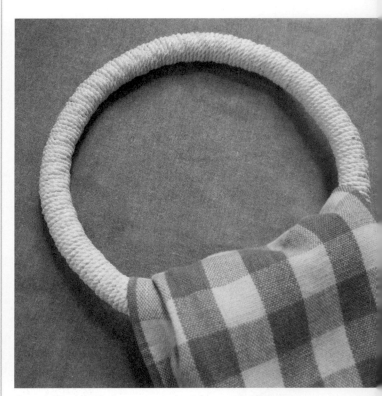

A manila towel ring covered with cotton twine.

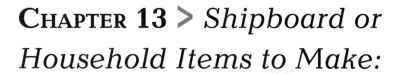

CHAPTER 13 > *Shipboard or Household Items to Make:*

Round Canvas Ditty Bag or Laundry Bag, Canvas Letter Holder, Rope Hammock

If you enjoy embellishing projects with colorful stitches and stamped accents, these projects are for you.

A finished hammock makes a marvelous island oasis in your backyard. Inset: A decorated round canvas bag and a canvas letter pouch—perfect gifts for your onboard neighbors.

Your local craft or hardware store contains all the materials you need to create a ditty bag, letter carrier, or hammock for between the masts or in your backyard.

1› Cut a rectangle from the canvas that's 11 inches tall and 21 inches long. Cut a circle from the canvas that's 7 inches in diameter.

2› Fold the canvas rectangle in half lengthwise and sew up the side with a hem of ½ inch (see cutting diagram).

3› On the canvas circle, draw a sewing line ½ inch in from the edge all the way around.

4› With your fingers, crease the material in the circle along the line.

5› On the inside of the tube of canvas, draw another sewing line ½ inch up from the bottom (see photo).

6› Insert the creased circle of material into the tube, matching

Round Canvas Bag/Ditty Bag

Here's a different kind of bag—it's round. Sailors often use bags like this, called ditty bags, to store odds and ends such as needles and small tools.

I kept the pattern for this bag on the small side (10 inches by 6 inches) so it can be completely sewn by hand. You can finish the bag fairly quickly. Make it bigger if you would like it to hold bigger objects; make it still bigger to serve as a clothing or laundry bag.

2-foot-square piece of canvas
3 to 4 feet of cotton cord for drawstring
sewing needle and heavy cotton thread
white glue
sharp knife or scissors
ruler
pencil
six ¼-inch (inside diameter) grommets
grommet-inserting tool (optional)
decorative fringe and colored threads

Follow these steps to create a ditty bag:

A ditty bag has many uses, both onshore and at sea.

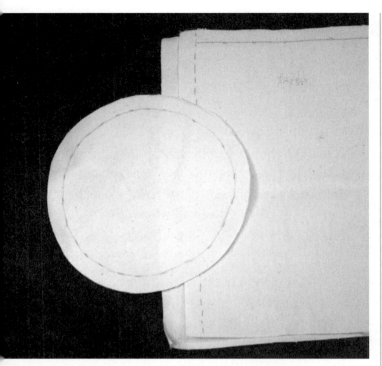

Sewing line drawn on circle and rectangle used to make the round canvas bag.

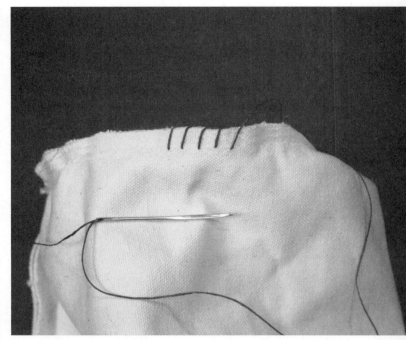

With the project inside out, sew the circle of canvas to the tube end.

the two sewing lines. Pin (or baste) and then sew the two pieces together with tight stitches, either by hand or machine (see photo).

7> Turn down a 2-inch hem on the inside of the top of the tube and sew it in place to stay.

Follow these steps to insert the drawstring into the ditty bag:

1> Turn the bag right side out and carefully measure where each grommet will sit.

2> Insert the six grommets by cutting out just enough fabric to insert the funnel side of the grommet into the material of the bag. Set the piece of material with the funnel side of the grommet onto the grommet tool.

3> Place the other part of the grommet over the funnel side and press the two sides of the grommet together with the tool. Repeat this process with each of the remaining grommets.

4> Weave the drawstring through the grommets to complete the basic round bag. Knot each end of the drawstring together so the ends don't come out of the grommets.

5> Your bag is now ready for you to add your own personal creativity with decorative fringe, colorful fabric markers, stitches, beads, or stamps.

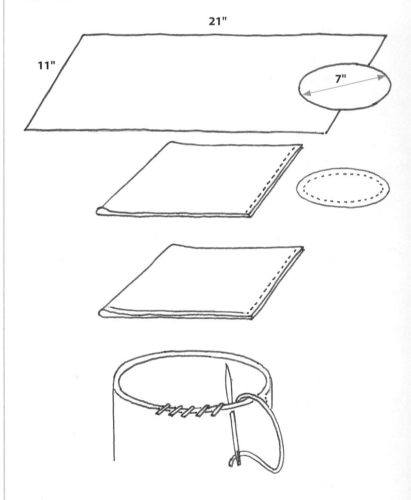

Cutting and sewing pieces for the ditty bag.

Canvas Letter Holder

This fancy snail-mail pouch is a way to show off your marlinspike skills when you are heading back to the boat from the post office. Or tie it to your favorite lounging chair as a holder for your remote controls.

18-inch by 12-inch piece of canvas
white glue
sewing needle and heavy cotton thread
cord for hanging
scissors
ruler
grommets and decorative flat knots (optional)

Follow these steps to create the canvas letter holder:

1› Pull out horizontal (weft) threads at the bottom 3 inches of the wide side of the canvas (you can pull out as much as 4 ½ inches depending on how you will use the fringe). Cut ½ inch of the vertical threads from the left and right sides of the flap.

2› Fold back the left side of the canvas ½ inch and sew it closed.

3› Fold the piece of canvas lengthwise in half so that its height is now 9 inches.

4› Fold the front piece of the canvas in half again to create a 4 ½-inch flap made of canvas and fringe.

5› Fold back the right side of the canvas ½ inch and sew it closed to make the pouch for the mail.

If you want to use grommets to hold your pouch, then follow these steps:

1› Fold back the top of the canvas ½ inch and sew it to create a neat hem.

2› Insert grommets in the top left and right corners of the pouch.

3› Now you can hang the pouch over hooks.

A letter holder can be decorated using a variety of knotting skills. The fringe shown here is alternating square knots.

The fringe has been created and the left side has been sewn for a nice clean edge.

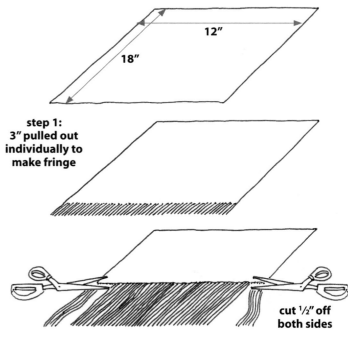

There are many ways to fold the canvas into a pouch. Shown here is a fold made for the pouch with a flap over it.

To make the mail pouch without grommets, follow these steps:

1> Lay the cord along the top of the canvas and fold about 1 inch of canvas over it.

2> Sew a seam along the canvas flap you created to hold the cord in place. Now you can tie the pouch between hooks.

3> In the fringed section you can use macramé. Sailors call it square knotting or McNamara's lace—as it is called in the navy.

4> Tie or glue other decorative knots to the front of the pouch, such as ocean plat knots (described in Chapter 7).

Three inches of weft have been pulled out individually, and ½ inch of the thread from the left and right sides have been removed. Cut ½ inch off both sides, and then fold and sew for a nice finished edge.

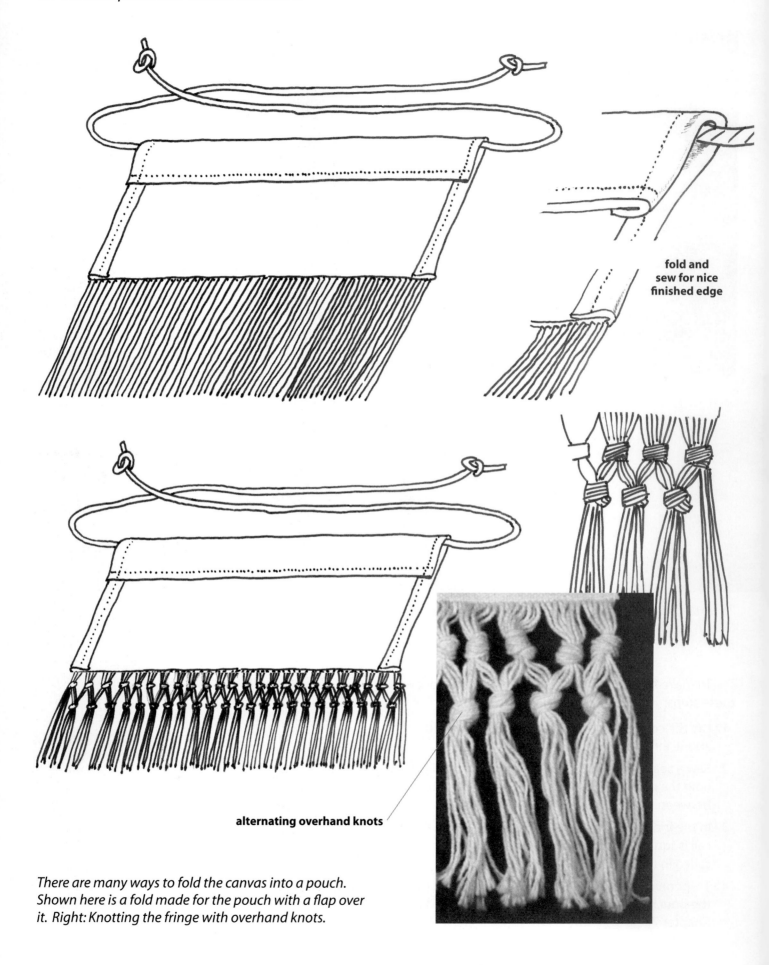

**fold and
sew for nice
finished edge**

alternating overhand knots

*There are many ways to fold the canvas into a pouch.
Shown here is a fold made for the pouch with a flap over
it. Right: Knotting the fringe with overhand knots.*

Rope Hammock

1,740 feet of ¼-inch cotton rope
two hammock spreader bars
two 3-inch-diameter rope grommets (carefully and correctly tied) or appropriate metal rings
masking tape
shellac (optional)
sharp knife or scissors
ruler

Some people think that a hammock is a piece of furniture. Well, this hammock is a piece of art.

Be warned that there is no fast way to do this project; you'll have to tie over 400 knots to complete this single-person hammock. Each of the knots must be tied the same size as its neighbor, and the rows of knots must alternate entry and exit points. That said, when you finish the hammock you will have a real masterpiece.

Follow these steps to tie the first hammock clew (the ropes that hold up the hammock):

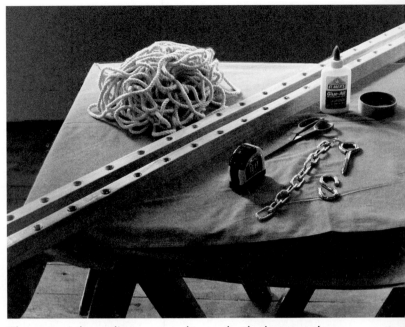

The material supplies you need to make the hammock are minimal—but you will need much time and a good dose of patience. Note that the hammock spreader bar shown here has twice as many holes as you need. You can leave the extra holes empty, or fill the holes with putty.

A finished hammock makes a marvelous island oasis in your backyard.

1› Cut five pieces of cotton rope, each 8 feet 6 inches long. Tape the ends or dip the ends in shellac to prevent them from unraveling.

2› Loop each piece of rope through the rope grommet or metal ring, creating ten strands that are each about 4 feet long.

3› Lay the grommet on a table. Pick up the first strand on the left, and in an over-under-over-under process draw this strand across the nine strands and out to the right (see photo and diagram).

4› Now pick up the strand on the right side and weave it over-under-over-under and out to the left (see photo and diagram).

The rope woven across the nine other strands.

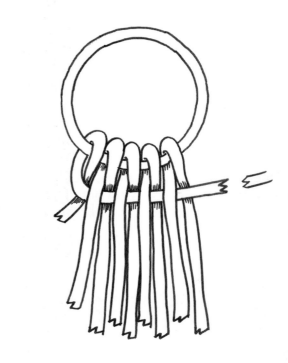

Weaving rope for the hammock clew.

The right strand woven through the other strands.

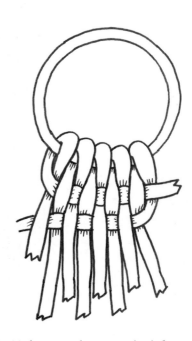

Weaving the right strand over to the left.

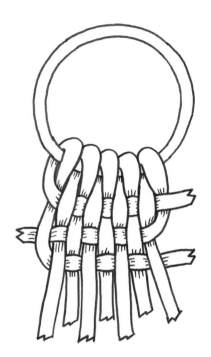

Weaving strands to create the hammock clew.

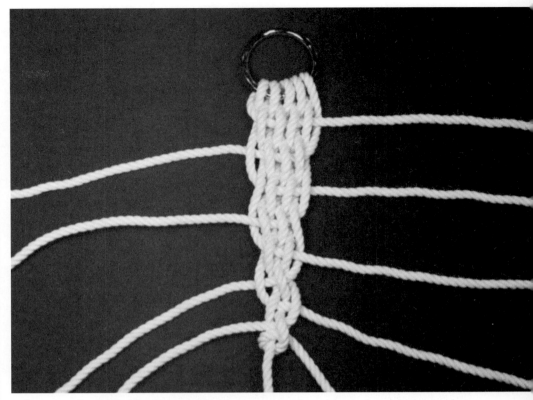

When the clew is finished, you will have ten strands ready to tie to the spreader bar.

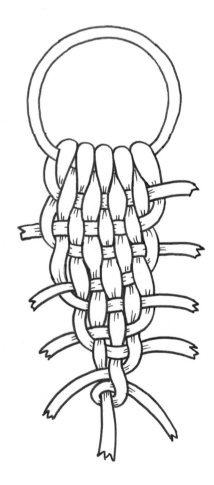

The completed hammock clew.

5> Continue this weaving process on the left and right sides until just two strands remain. Tie an overhand knot with these two strands. (See diagram and photo.)

6> Lace the ten ends of the clew through the spreader bar. My bar measures 4 feet by 1⅜ inches by 1 inch, with ten holes drilled through about every 5 inches. (If your pre-purchased spreader bar has more than ten holes, you can fill them with wood putty.) Set your bars aside, but not too far away.

Follow these steps to make the body of the hammock:

1> Cut twenty lengths of cotton cord, each 41 feet long.

2> Find the middle of the first two long cords, and holding these cords in the middle bring the end of the first clew strand that exits the spreader bar to it. Tie a bowline with the clew strand around the middle of the pair of long cords (see diagram).

3> Continue tying the clew ropes to the middled (folded in half) pairs of hammock ropes until all twenty lengths are tied in place.

4> Now tie the first row of carrick bend knots as shown in the diagram (see Chapter 7 to learn how to tie a carrick bend). Note that each knot is tied close to the next one, and the entry and exit points are the same all the way across the row.

5> Tie each carrick bend in the second row close to its neighbor. Make sure that the entry and exit points for the knots in the second row are exactly opposite from those in the row above.

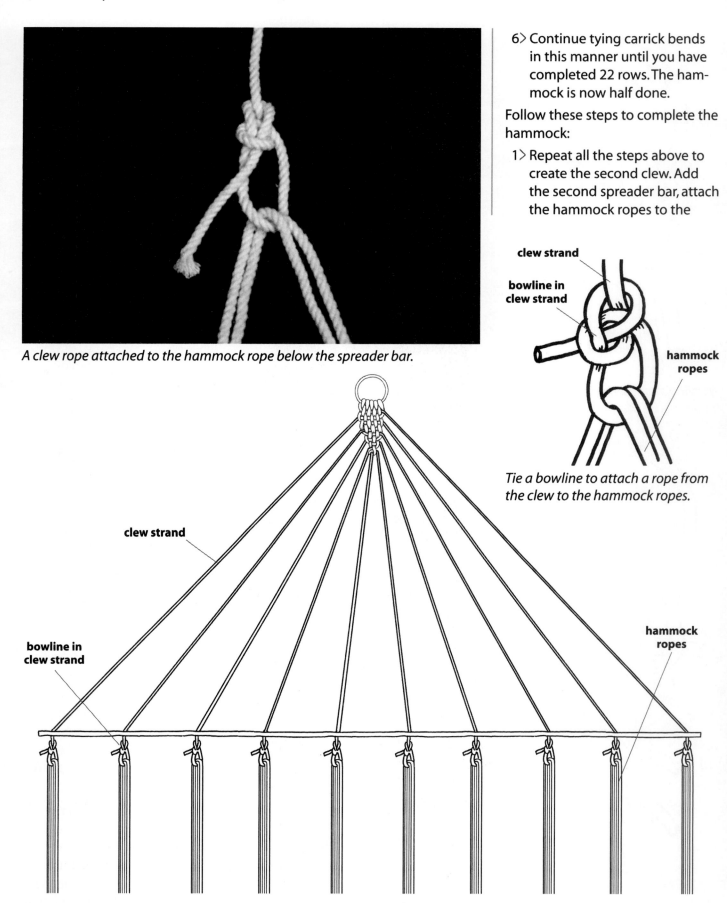

A clew rope attached to the hammock rope below the spreader bar.

6> Continue tying carrick bends in this manner until you have completed 22 rows. The hammock is now half done.

Follow these steps to complete the hammock:

1> Repeat all the steps above to create the second clew. Add the second spreader bar, attach the hammock ropes to the

clew strand

bowline in clew strand

hammock ropes

Tie a bowline to attach a rope from the clew to the hammock ropes.

clew strand

bowline in clew strand

hammock ropes

The clew ropes attached to the hammock ropes.

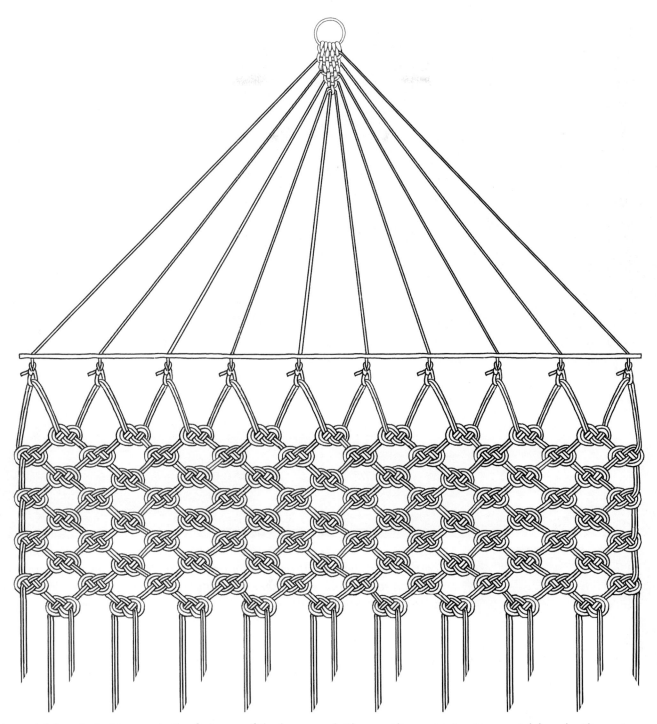

Nine carrick bends tied to create the first row of the hammock. The next line contains ten carrick bends. Alternate rows of nine and ten carrick bends for a full hammock.

clew ropes, and complete 21 rows of carrick bends in the body of the hammock.

2> Now it's time to connect the two halves of the hammock together. Follow these steps:

3> Leave a tail of about 8 inches at the end of the last row of carrick bends for each half of the hammock (cut off any excess rope).

4> Lay both sides of the hammock on a table so that the ends meet in the middle.

5> Starting with the first pair of carrick bends that meet in the middle, tie the tails together using overhand knots close and tight to the carrick bends to make the seam. The knots are tied so they are on the underside of the hammock.

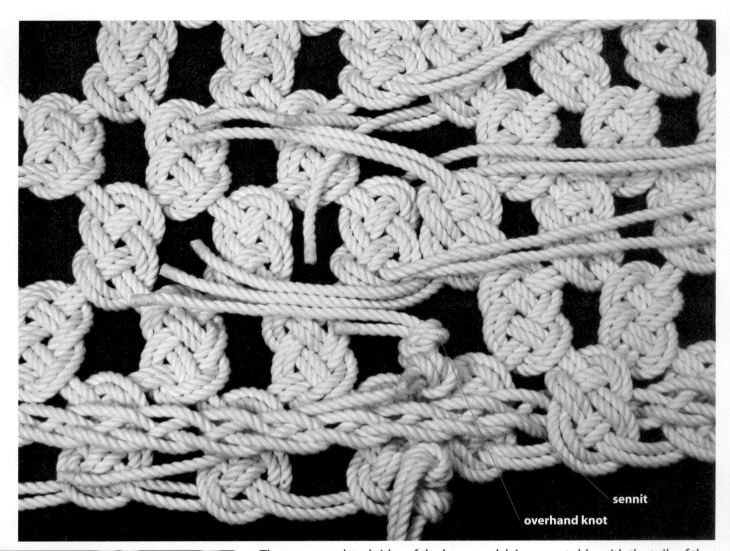

sennit

overhand knot

overhand knot

overhand knot

The two completed sides of the hammock lying on a table, with the tails of the carrick bends being tied with overhand knots on the bottom of the hammock. You can see the four-strand sennit (see instructions) being woven into the edge of the hammock in the photo. The close-up (at left) shows how closely the overhand knots are tied to the carrick bends.

To complete the hammock, you need to make a strap (four-strand sennit—see Chapter 9) for both long sides of the hammock. This gives the hammock a nice finished edge, and when tensioned a small amount provides a gentle "belly" to the hammock.

1> Take two pieces of ¼-inch cotton rope, each 18 feet long. Middle them (fold them in half) and with the four strands braid a nice sennit 6 feet long. You'll need to leave tails of about 10 inches to tie off.

2> To install the strap, find the first bowline at the head of the hammock at the left. Untie the bowline and then add the bight and re-tie the bowline so that it holds the first bight of the carrick bend and the bight of the strap.

3> Weave the strand in and out down the side (see photo).

4> When you reach the foot of the hammock, tie the ends into the corresponding carrick bend bight.

This hammock is designed

for one person, whose weight should not exceed 225 pounds. The first time you sit in the hammock, it will stretch as much as 12 inches, so be careful as you sit.

Note that spinning or swinging in the hammock is not recommended. The ropes might loosen, which might result in injury.

rim draw-up strap

The sennit strap you created for a nice finished edge is shown here getting inserted into the bowline of the clew strand.

Glossary

Terms in **bold** are also defined in this glossary.

Ashley's flat knot A woven knot (also known as Ashley's #2216) made of one or more **strand**s that can be tightened to decorate round or cylindrical objects.

Bend A knot used to join two ropes.

Bight A loop in a length of rope.

Bitter end The nonworking end of a line.

Canvas A tough off-white colored fabric woven from threads of **cotton**.

Carrick bend A knot used to tie two different ropes together. Its design is similar to that of a **square knot**.

Chafe To wear or fray a rope.

Chinese button knot A knot used as a button or used to make decorative items such as bracelets.

Clove hitch A knot used to attach a rope to an object. A clove hitch wraps around the object, with the **bitter end** and the **working end** going in opposite directions.

Clover A loop tied in a decorative knot, also known as a bight.

Coil A neat circles of rope, piled to keep the loops free of tangles.

Construction Refers to the design of rope, including the number of **strand**s, and the arrangement of each in the strands.

Cord Refers to small sizes of ropes.

Cordage A rope or ropelike material varying in size from **twine** to hawser; in nautical handiwork, rope of less than ½ inch (12 mm) diameter, or **small stuff**.

Cotton A member of the mallow family. When the flower goes to seed, long fibers or staples are formed to protect the seed and help the seeds when they are eventually dispersed on the wind.

Cotton seine twine Twine made from up to 120 threads of cotton.

Crown knot A knot used to make buttons and other items. Often combined with a **wall knot**.

Diameter The distance measured through the center of a cross section of rope or cordage. For noncritical use, determine the diameter by measuring the rope's circumference, or girth, and divide by three.

Drawn fringe lace Needlework consisting of two stages.

Eye A loop spliced at the end of a rope.

Granny knot A **square knot** tied incorrectly.

Grommet A ring of wood, rope, or metal.

Hitch A knot used to tie **cordage** around a hook, ring, or (in a decorative fashion) around an object such as a handle or tube.

Hockle A condition whereby a rope **strand** twists on itself: also called a chinkle.

Kink A tight **hockle** that upsets the lay of a rope: a sharp bend that permanently distorts the strands.

Knot A weak substitute for a **splice**, but easy to unfasten.

Lace Highly decorated fabric. Used to embellish clothing or household items.

Lanyard A length of **small stuff**, sometimes decorative, tied to an object to make it secure.

Lark's head knot A knot made by looping cordage or rope around an object and pulling the ends through the loop. Also called a cow hitch.

Lash To secure with rope.

Lay The direction of the twists in a rope **strand** (see right-laid) that are helically laid into rope.

Leather The skin of various animals, chemically treated in various ways to color, soften, and preserve.

Macramé From the Arabic work *migramah* (ornamental fringe). It first appeared as decorative knotting in the unfinished warp threads in Middle Eastern linens.

Manila cordage/rope Rope composed of fibers grown in the Philippines, specifically the abaca plant.

Marry To interlace two ropes, end to end, for splicing.

McNamara's lace An intricate style of knots tied in canvas fringe. Invented by sailors in the U.S. Navy.

Middle, middling To fold a piece of **cordage** in half.

Net knot A knot used to create nets and hammocks.

Ocean plat knot A knot that is a variation on a **carrick bend**, used to make flat mats.

Pure grain alcohol A 190-proof grain spirit. Clear, flammable liquid distilled from grain mesh to a very high percentage of ethanol.

Rayon Manufactured from whets of cellulose (white crumb). The **cordage** imitates silk and is easily dyed.

Reeve To pass the end of a rope through a hole.

Right-laid A rope with strands twisted up and to the right when the end points away from the viewer.

Seize To securely bind the end of a rope or strand with **small stuff**.

Sennit Braided **cordage**.

Serve To cover the surface of a line or wire with a smooth wrapping of fiber cord.

Shellac A quick-drying finish/sealer. Cultivated from the cast-off cocoon of the *Laccifer lacca* beetle.

Small stuff Rope of less than ½ inch (12 mm) diameter.

Splice The interweaving of two ends of ropes so as to make a continuous or endless length without appreciably increasing the diameter; making a loop, or an **eye**, in the end of a rope by tucking the ends of the **strand**s.

Square knot A knot based on half-knots that joins two pieces of **cordage** or rope.

Standing part The area in the rope that is inactive, as opposed to the working end, **bitter end**, or **bight**.

Strand An arrangement of fibers or wires helically laid about an axis to produce a symmetrical section.

Tuck To push a single **strand** through the body of a rope.

Turk's Head knot A braided knot made from a series of **strand**s and **clover**s. These knots can be made flat or bound around a cylinder such as a spar.

Twine Rope of a diameter larger than a sewing thread but smaller than a shoelace.

Unlay To take the twist out of a three-strand rope. The ends of the three **strand**s are taped to prevent them from unlaying.

Wall knot A knot used to make buttons and other items. Often combined with a **crown knot**.

Whip To wrap the end of a rope with **small stuff** to prevent the rope from **unlay**ing.

Working end The part of **cordage** used to create a knot.

Working load A manufacturer's recommendation of the maximum pounds of pull to which a rope can safely be subjected—generally, one-tenth the new rope's breaking strength.

Yarn A group of fibers twisted together; thread.

Acknowledgments

I HAVE BEEN KNOTTING AND TYING FOR DECADES and all I know about this subject has been said before by many other teachers, writers, sailors, and artists. I would like to thank all those who have gone before me, for their knowledge, patience, and generosity in teaching me. I would also like to thank all my clients, be they sailors or boaters or others, who have pushed me to find clever ways to create items for them.

A special note of thanks to: my editor, Molly Mulhern; illustrator Ben Martinez; and photographer Dave Dawson.

Index

Create more projects for both land and sea through the art of rope splicing

THE SPLICING HANDBOOK

THIRD EDITION

Techniques for Traditional and Modern Ropes and Wires

Barbara Merry with John Darwin

978-0-07-173604-6 • $20.00
Available in print and eBook